LISTENING TO CHILDREN

The professional response to hearing the abused child

Anne Bannister, Kevin Barrett, Eileen Shearer

Longman Group UK Ltd, 6th Floor
Westgate House, The High, Harlow, Essex CM20 1YR

© Longman Group UK Ltd 1990
© Khadj Rouf, chapter 1
© Eileen Shearer, chapter 7

All rights reserved. No part of this publication may be reproduced, stored in a retrieval system, or transmitted in any form or by any means, electronic, mechanical, photocopying, recording or otherwise, without the prior permission of the Copyright owner or a licence permitting restricted copying issued by the Copyright Licensing Agency Ltd., 33-34 Alfred Place, London WC1E 7DP.

British Library Cataloguing in Publication Data
Listening to children.
1. Social services. Personnel. Communication with children
I. Bannister, Anne; II Barrett, Kevin; III Shearer, Eileen.
361.32083

ISBN 0-582-07566-1

Typeset by EMS Phototypesetting, Hide Hill,
Berwick upon Tweed, Northumberland.

Printed and bound in Great Britain
by Dotesios Printers Ltd, Trowbridge, Wiltshire.

Contents

List of Contributors — v

Acknowledgements — viii

Foreword   Christopher Brown, Director of the National Society for the Prevention of Cruelty to Children — ix

Introduction   Anne Bannister, Kevin Barrett and Eileen Shearer — xi
1. My self in echoes. My voice in song
   Khadj Rouf — 1

PART 1 — CHILDREN IN SOCIETY
2. Children in society: *children as possessions — and millstones, children in poverty, new babies in the decade*
   Penelope Leach — 20
3. Listening to children and representing them — a lawyer's view
   Michael D. A. Freeman — 30

PART 2 — AGENCIES WHICH SERVE CHILDREN
4. Telling tales: in and out of school: *the school as a listening community; the school nurse's role*
   Michael Marland and Gill Malcolm — 40
5. Active listening — a social services' perspective: *statutory duties in Local Authority social work and listening to children, listening to children and working with families, ways of listening, the emotional impact of listening to children*
   Jan Thurgood — 51
6. A permanent mark? — management responsibility in child protection work: *the welfare net, professional responsibilities, personal difficulties, staff care, providing quality service, professional networks, mirroring families, the importance of listening*
   Murray Davies — 68

PART 3 — PROTECTING THE ABUSED CHILD: CHILD PROTECTION INVESTIGATION

7. Child abuse investigation — tuning in to the child's world: *Jane's story, workers rights — the foundation of investigations, initial referral, seeing the family, conclusion*
   Eileen Shearer — 84
8. Learning to listen to children: *Staff selection and training, visual aids and hindrances, how do we listen to children, the setting — permission to speak, ways of listening, interviewing the child, staff training, conclusion*
   Euan M. Ross — 100
9. Persuading the courts to listen to children: *discovering the child's wishes in civil proceedings, obtaining evidence from children about disputed matters of fact, competency, open court, the hearsay rule, rules about corroboration, reform in sight? the proposals of the Pigot Committee, conclusion*
   J. R. Spencer — 110

PART 4 — THERAPY FOR THE ABUSED CHILD

10. Listening to, talking to and understanding children – reality, imagination, dreams and fantasy: *definitions of abuse, the child in context, the setting, meeting the child, unstructured and structured period, understanding the communications of children, particular issues and examples*
    Judith Trowell — 124
11. 'Why should I talk to you?' Initial interviews with distressed adolescents
    Paul Holmes — 140
12. Listening and learning: psychodramatic techniques with children: *communicating, learning, the inner voice, awareness*
    Anne Bannister — 155

PART 5 — THE WAY FORWARD

13. Towards a child-friendly society: *making a place for parenting, parent-friendly professionals, a new look at daycare dilemmas, children's rights, children's needs for privileged parents, putting parents and children first*
    Penelope Leach — 172

The chapters in this book reflect the practice, experience and views of the authors and do not necessarily reflect or express NSPCC policy.

List of contributors

Anne Bannister Anne Bannister is a social worker and psychotherapist, registered as a Dramatherapist and a Psychodramatist. She manages the Child Sexual Abuse Consultancy in Manchester for the NSPCC and has specialised in child abuse work, especially sexual abuse, for the last ten years. She has published many articles in the professional press and is the author of chapters in *Child Abuse and Neglect — Facing the Challenge*, Eds. Wendy Stainton-Rodgers, Denise Heavey and Elizabeth Ash., The Open University, 1989.; *Child Sexual Abuse*, Eds. Blagg, Hughes and Wattam. Longman, 1989; and *Psychodrama: Inspiration and Technique*, Routledge, 1990. She is a co-editor of this book.

Kevin Barrett Kevin Barrett was educated at Middlesex Polytechnic, University of London and Oxford University. He has practised in London as a residential and field social worker. For the last five years he has worked as a Policy Officer for the NSPCC.

Eileen Shearer Eileen Shearer has been a social worker for 16 years and qualified at Oxford University in 1978. She was a local authority senior social worker for five years before joining Rochdale, Oldham and Bury NSPCC CPT and in 1989 she became a Team Manager. She has co-written *We all get Stressed: A Survival Manual for Helpers*, NSPCC, 1989 and 'Making Sense of Sexual Abuse: Charting the Shifting Sands' in *Child Sexual Abuse*, Eds. Blagg, Hughes and Wattam, Longman, 1989. She has also written an article entitled 'Issues for Treatment Work with Families', published in *Context*, Association of Family Therapy Journal. She is a co-editor of this book.

Murray Davies Murray Davies qualified in Applied Social Studies and Social Work at Dundee University in 1972. Before his appointment as Team Manager in Rochdale, he had worked in Social Services Departments in England and Scotland. In 1985 he was appointed NSPCC Regional Social Work Manager, with responsibility for NSPCC services in Greater Manchester and Cheshire. He has published papers and booklets on child protection issues, and is a co-author of *Dangerous Families* (1986). He is also an external practice assessor to the Post Qualifying Course in Child Protection at Lancaster University, and an advisor to the Department of Health London on child protection training. He is currently the Regional Child Care Director for Wales and the West Midlands of England.

Michael D. A. Freeman Michael Freeman is a barrister and Professor of English Law at University College London. He has written extensively on family law and on children's rights, including *The Rights and Wrongs of Children*, Frances Pinter 1983.

Paul Holmes Paul Holmes is an adolescent psychiatrist, psychodramatist and individual psychotherapist. From 1984 to 1989 he was a consultant in Wandsworth, London where he founded ACT, the Wandsworth Adolescent Community Team, which provides a service for disturbed 14 to 19 year olds. He is now developing his interest in writing, psychodrama, teaching and consultation work in England and Mexico City (where he is based for eight months of the year). He has recently co-edited with Marcia Karp a book, *Psychodrama: Inspiration and Technique*, Routledge, 1990. His own book on psychodrama and psychoanalytic theory will be published in 1991.

Penelope Leach Penelope Leach followed a first degree in history at Cambridge University with a diploma in social work and then a PhD in psychology from the University of London. After ten years of academic research into many aspects of child development, the birth of her own children made her conscious of the gulf between professionals and parents, theory and practice. It is this gulf she has tried to bridge in books like *Babyhood* (Penguin, revised in 1983) *Baby and Child*, now in its second million and in 29 languages (new edition for the 1990s, Penguin 1989) and *The Babypack*, a pop-up book for new parents published in 1990 (Jonathan Cape). Penelope is a Fellow of the British Psychological Society and a Vice President of the Health Visitors' Association. She has worked for parents organisations concerned with pre-school education, day-care and pre-natal education and is closely associated with the NSPCC and its sister organisations in the United States, Canada and Ireland. Her current research is with a national study of adolescents (*Youthscan*) and she is parent education coordinator for the campaign to End Physical Punishment Of Children (EPOCH).

Gill Malcolm Gill Malcolm has worked in Tower Hamlets for the past ten years, and is currently working as Nurse Specialist in Child Protection and as a Child Protection Advisor for School Nurses. She has been involved in setting up a North East Thames Regional School Nurse Group and has also been closely involved with the setting up and evaluation of a Child Protection Advisors project in

List of contributors

Tower Hamlets.

Michael Marland Michael Marland has been Headteacher of North Westminster Community School since 1980. He is General Editor of the Heinemann Organisation in Schools Series, which includes his own *Pastoral Care*, 1979, *Language Across the Curriculum*, 1977 and *School Management Skills*, 1986. He was the founder-chair of the National Association for Pastoral Care in Education, and has contributed to professional development extensively in this field. He was made CBE in the Jubilee Honours of 1977 and has been honorary Professor of Education at Warwick University since 1980.

Professor Euan M. Ross Professor Ross holds the Chair in Community Paediatrics at King's College, London and is also honorary consultant in community paediatrics to Camberwell, one of England's most deprived health districts. Professor Ross has worked in child health since 1964 and has seen child abuse become increasingly recognised and emerge as a major part of child health work in the UK. His other medical interests include the causation, recognition and management of child handicap.

Khadj Rouf Khadj Rouf, born in 1968, is a survivor of child sexual abuse. She has written a paper, 'Journey through Darkness' *Child Sexual Abuse* Vol. 6 (1) 1989, and is the co-author with Anne Peake, of *Working with Sexually Abused Children: A Resource Pack for Professionals*, The Children's Society, 1989. Khadj Rouf is currently studying psychology at Oxford University.

John Spencer John Spencer is a Lecturer in Law at Cambridge University and a Fellow of Selwyn College. He specialises in criminal procedure and evidence. Since 1986 he has taken a particular interest in the evidence of children on which with Rhona Flin he has recently written the book *The Evidence of Children — the Law and the Psychology*, Blackstone Press Ltd, 1990.

Jan Thurgood Jan Thurgood is a team Leader at Westminster Children's Hospital, Westminster City Social Services Department. She has previously worked for the London Borough of Wandsworth as a field social worker and as Deputy Officer in Charge of a Day Assessment Centre for children and adolescents. Her major practice interests are in direct work with children and family work.

Judith Trowell Judith Trowell is a consultant psychiatrist and Chair of the Child and Family Department at the Tavistock Clinic. She is an Honorary Consultant at the Royal Free Hospital, a psychoanalyst and child analyst and psychiatric advisor to the NSPCC. She has learned most about children from her son and daughter.

Acknowledgements

The publishers are indebted to K. Armstrong for permission to use an extract of an article in *Caring* (1981) **7**, 2; Elizabeth Ash *Acceptable Risk* (1988) CCEBW; Virginia Axline *Play Therapy* (1989) Ballantine Books; P. Dale, M. Davies, A. Morrison and J. Waters *Dangerous Families* (1986) Routledge; R. Greenwood *The Technique and Practice of Psychoanalysis* (1967) Hogarth; R. E. Helfer and C. H. Kempe (Eds.) *Child Abuse and Neglect: the family and the community* (1976) Ballinger; Lord Justice Butler-Sloss *Report of the Enquiry into Child Abuse in Cleveland 1987* (1988) Her Majesty's Stationery Office; *The Children Act 1989* HMSO; Keri Hulme *The Bone People* (1985) Spiral & Hodder & Stoughton; A. Kakabadse, R. Ludlow and S. Vinnicombe *Working in Organisations* (1988) Penguin; C. Mastach and A. Pines for an article in *Child Care Quarterly* ; Alice Miller *The Drama of Being a Child* (1983) Virago and *For Your Own Good: The roots of violence in child rearing* (1985) Virago; D. A. Mrazek and P. B. Mrazek in P. B. Mrazek and C. H. Kempe's *Sexually Abused Children and Their Families* (1981) Pergammon; J. Oakland *Total Quality Management* (1989) Heinemann; V. Oaklander *Windows to our Children* (1978) Real People Press; Plato *The Republic* Penguin edition (1955); Jacqueline Spring *Cry Hard and Swim* (1987) Virago; Rosa Waugh *The Life of Benjamin Waugh* (1913) T. Fisher Unwin.

Foreword

Listening can seem a deceptively simple activity which in practice often proves notoriously difficult. Few of us would admit that at times we do not listen to our children and probably fewer would recognise that when we do listen we may not always hear what they are trying to tell us. Listening to children is not a simple or straightforward activity and listening to children who have been abused requires particular skills on the part of the professionals involved. The quality of professional decision making is heavily dependent upon how well professionals listen.

The last year has seen a number of important developments relating to the welfare and the rights of children. The ratification of the United Nations Convention on the Rights of the Child, the Report of the Pigot inquiry on Video Recorded evidence and the Children Act have all in their different ways embodied the idea that children not only have the right to express their views but also to have their views heard and considered.

The implementation of the Children Act and the UN Convention of the Rights of the Child will have a crucial effect on professional practice and the extent to which professionals will be able to listen to children. As ever resources play a pivotal role and without adequate funding such measures will inevitably fail. It is for child care professionals from the statutory and voluntary sectors to press the government to ensure that both the Children Act and the UN Convention are effectively implemented and monitored.

The idea for a book on the theme of Listening to Children originated out of a symposium on the subject held during the NSPCC's Listening to Children Week in 1989. A second Listening to Children Week was held by the NSPCC in October 1990 as part of the NSPCC's continuing campaign to raise awareness of the importance of listening and bring about changes in public attitudes towards children. Only when children are accorded the respect and the rights normally enjoyed by adults will they be treated as what they are — people in their own right.

Written for professionals this book explores the complexities of listening to vulnerable or damaged children from a range of perspectives. *Listening to Children: The Professional Response to Hearing the Abused Child* comes as a timely reminder to professionals that listening and hearing what children are saying is fundamental not only to the rights of children but also to their protection.

Christopher Brown
Director, NSPCC
September 1990

Introduction
Anne Bannister, Kevin Barrett, Eileen Shearer

> For their development children need the respect and protection of adults who take them seriously, love them, and honestly help them to become oriented in the world. — Alice Miller, *The Untouched Key: Tracing Childhood Trauma in Creativity and Destructiveness*, 1990, Virago.

When it stated that 'children are people and not objects of concern' the Cleveland Inquiry Report (1988) articulated an important if self-evident truth that children are people, with rights. It is interesting that the statement (which received a minor mention in the Report itself) needed to be made at all, and that it subsequently so caught the imagination of public and professionals. It is still not uncommon for the attitude that 'children should be seen and not heard' to be expressed if not explicitly then in deed or sentiment.

Professionals do not work in isolation and working against a social backdrop where many children are still too often treated as possessions is not only difficult but also abusive to children. In a multi-racial, multi-cultural society our social system is not sufficiently aware of the problems raised by language and cultural difference. To listen to children whose language or culture is different from our own is a task requiring extra preparation and thought. Communication with children with disabilities will also be frustrating both to the worker and child, and even abusive, unless the worker recognises his own limitations and acknowledges the problems. A deaf child or one with learning disabilities can communicate: we must take the responsibility to understand. Only when all adults learn to listen to them will children be treated with the dignity and respect they deserve as people.

The United Nations' Convention on the Rights of the Child and to a lesser extent, the Children Act (1989) provide a framework for protecting and implementing children's rights. Both embody the principle that children have the right, not only to express their opinions and feelings, but also that these should be taken into account when decisions are taken about their lives. While both the UN Convention and the Children Act are very important developments they do not in themselves guarantee that children will be heard and the attitudes of parents and children will ultimately determine whether children are given a voice.

Within the context of working with children who have been abused the availability of resources will be a critical issue. Without training professionals will not develop the skills to listen and without time and adequate staffing levels they will not have the opportunity to use their skills. The development of sensitive, high quality services will be undermined by a lack of adequate funding.

Listening is essential to communication and for professionals involved in child protection, the process of listening to children is fundamental to their effectiveness in protecting children from abuse and in preventing them from becoming 'objects of concern'. Listening is not an optional activity and failure to hear what children are trying to say is a denial of their basic human rights and also extremely dangerous. Failure to listen effectively can result in abuse or re-abuse, sometimes with fatal consequences.

Listening to children and actually hearing what they are trying to say is not necessarily the same activity. Listening is an active process the success of which can be influenced by many factors. The age and understanding of the child (not the same thing), the setting, prior events, the type of abuse can all affect how a child tells their story. Mutual trust is an essential component in communicating effectively. Children must trust the person to whom they are telling their story and the professional must always take seriously what the child is saying.

In her two chapters Penelope Leach describes the social context in which children live — one in which their needs are often undervalued. In 'Children in Society' she shows how children remain a low priority in a society where parenthood and child care remain peripheral to the mainstream activity of wealth creation. Social and economic policies benefit the few while the needs of children and families remain un-met. In 'Towards a Child-Friendly Society' she explores how public attitudes and child care policies need to change to permit a more child-friendly and parent-friendly society which reflects the real values of children and parents.

The importance of listening cannot be better illustrated than by looking at the consequences of failing to hear what children are saying themselves. In her chapter 'My self in echoes. My voice in song' Khadj Rouf recounts her personal experiences of incest and

Introduction

describes the betrayal of trust, the feelings of pain, fear and disgust that she felt as a child, much of which could have been avoided if adults had listened. Her personal courage has enabled Rouf to survive the horrific experiences of her childhood. It is salutary to remind ourselves that many do not.

Ensuring the rights of children who have been abused requires that all professions they come into contact with during the child protection process (legal, medical, education, etc.) have the skills to listen.

The role of lawyers in representing children in the court process is pivotal in protecting children and in his chapter 'Listening to children and representing them — a lawyer's view', Michael Freeman outlines the difficulties, both conceptual and practical that lawyers face when representing children. Does representation mean representing the child's wishes or their best interest? Are lawyers fact-finders, advocates or both? He identifies a number of roles lawyers adopt and describes the skills lawyers need, but so often lack, to listen, talk to and represent children effectively.

Schools have a central part to play in identifying abuse and getting help for the abused child. In 'Telling tales: in and out of school', Michael Marland and Gill Malcolm discuss the difficulties which even child-focused institutions such as schools seem to present when it comes to listening to children. Marland makes a plea for well trained, pastoral care teachers who can operate within an accepted and well-resourced structure in schools in partnership with parents. Malcolm points out the opportunities the school nurse can present to the unhappy or abused child as a source of refuge, help and understanding. She describes the skills needed to encourage the child to talk and to listen.

Jan Thurgood's chapter 'Active listening — a social services' perspective', stresses the point that other authors raise: listening is a dynamic process, not a passive one. She also adds meaning to the word 'co-operation', the lack of which is mentioned time and again in reports into child deaths. The nursery staff, the school, the parents, all have valuable information about the child which must be listened to. Thurgood reminds us that the Social Worker's task is to make sense of all this information in the light of the child's own words and behaviour.

Murray Davies argues in his chapter 'A permanent mark? — management responsibility in child protection work' that high quality services for abused children and their families are dependent on the quality of professional supervision given to front line workers by their managers, and on the degree to which healthy communication, and 'active listening' exists within our organisations. He emphasises the importance of the professional network in effectively protecting children, and the need to recognise the process of mirroring between families, workers and organisations. Active listening is essential in every arena if the children are to be heard.

In 'Child abuse investigation — tuning in to the child's world', Eileen Shearer illuminates the key position played by those who investigate allegations of abuse. She uses the metaphor of 'tuning in' to the child's voice. Investigation is always a stressful procedure for everyone involved. Strong, powerful, adult voices demand to be heard. The weaker child's voice can be expressing acute pain which workers may find hard to bear. Shearer cuts a swathe through distractions and irrelevancies and clarifies what investigative workers need to know and to do in order to protect children.

The medical examination is a crucial point in the detection of child abuse. In 'Learning to listen to children' Euan Ross describes the difficulties which face members of the medical profession in listening to children: lack of training, lack of understanding within the wider profession, lack of child-centred resources. He goes on to describe a structured method of interviewing children and offers suggestions to enable them to reveal themselves.

The trauma of appearing in court and the fear of confronting the alleged abuser can undermine or prevent children telling their story. Rules governing the competency of child witnesses and the corroboration of evidence can equally inhibit natural justice. John Spencer explores these issues in his chapter 'Persuading the courts to listen to children' and outlines the Pigot Inquiry (1989) recommendations which would go a considerable way to preventing the secondary abuse of children in criminal court proceedings.

Anne Bannister describes her work with abused children and the need to identify with the child in order to really hear and help the child deal with the horrors he/she has experienced. She details particular techniques which can be used in this demanding work and gives examples of psychodrama with such children.

In allowing us to listen to his own feelings Paul Holmes mirrors the way in which he listens to the feelings of his young patients. Sensitive to their vulnerability, he recognises his own. His strength lies in his willingness to take seriously everything the young person says or does and this, of course, is the essence of good listening. He 'listens' to what is being stated, obliquely perhaps, by the behaviour of the adolescent who sulks, stays out late or runs away.

In her chapter 'Listening to, talking to and understanding children', Judith Trowell pursues a similar theme to Holmes. From her perspective as a psychiatrist and child analyst, she helps us to understand the messages the child is giving in her behaviour. The trust which she develops between herself and her young patients is obvious and we see how this enables her to listen to sad and

Introduction

vulnerable children.

The function of listening changes as investigation moves on to treatment and the need for evidence gives way to the need for therapy; nevertheless the quality of listening remains of prime importance to the child. Some professionals do not have the necessary skills to listen, others will lack the personal resources to listen and confront painful and disturbing accounts of abuse. A combination of professional skills and personal qualities are needed to listen effectively.

Listening and hearing the abused child is the foundation of effective child protection. Listening determines not only the quality of the decisions professionals make about children's lives (which can have such profound consequences) but also the extent to which professionals can heal the harm caused to children by abuse and avoid compounding such harm in a well meaning but insensitive professional response.

If children are to enjoy the rights accorded to them changes are needed in the way society treats children and the attitudes many adults hold towards children. In the child protection context improvements in how professionals listen to children must be followed by policy, organisational and procedural changes which reflect the changes in practice and provide genuinely child-centred services. The political will must also be forthcoming if the resources are to be provided to allow this to happen.

Listening to children whether as a relative, a friend, a parent or a professional is the foundation upon which we can give children their rights as people and ensure their voice is heard.

1 My self in echoes. My voice in song

Khadj Rouf ©

Hello! I'm Khadj. Glad to meet you. Sorry my room is a tip. I meant to tidy up for your coming round but I had an essay to do and then I panicked because I couldn't remember where I'd left my photo album. Turned out to be under a pile of books that should have been returned to the library two weeks ago! Sit down, please. Tea or Coffee? Coffee. Sugar, Milk! Okay!

I picked up my photos from home when I went back for the holidays. I had a feeling you'd be in Oxford soon so I thought I'd break the habit of a lifetime and not leave it until the last minute to get it all sorted.

I know you want me to go into my past for your chapter.

Here's your coffee. Some biscuits there.

Oh, don't apologise. I'm used to it now. It is still upsetting sometimes but I want to help other children who are suffering now. *And* help other people understand. God! I always feel so outdated when I say that. Wanting to help other people seems to have gone out of fashion these days.

Well. This is my Mum when she was sixteen. Really pretty isn't she? Mad hair style though — must have taken *ages* for her hair to do that! And this is my Dad when he was about nineteen. The photo is really bad but it must be about forty years old. He was a lot older than Mum.

This is their wedding day. They got married in a registry office. Nobody came from either family.

All my Dad's relatives were back home in Bangladesh. I'm not sure he even told them he was getting married until after he'd done it. No-one came from Mum's side either. There was a big stigma about mixed marriages in the 'Sixties. It wasn't the done thing. A white woman who married a black man was considered to have moved into the gutter. Few steps up from a sewer rat. And this is me. I was born exactly a year after they married. I was such an ugly baby! And the *size* of the nappy! Mum didn't have much experience about putting nappies on babies then. That accounts for it going up to my armpits, I think.

I obviously don't remember any of this stuff. I think we lived in Toxteth then, and we moved when I was about a year old.

Here's me when I was about four with my baby brother. Those were my best clothes. I remember them really vaguely. I don't remember this photo being taken either. Look pretty gormless don't I? I bet my Mum struggled to get me to look at the camera for ages and look at me, looking the other way! I'd probably seen something really enthralling like an empty crisp packet!

This is me when I was five. Standing next to Mum. She's wearing the sari she got married in. It looks really beautiful. I'm so short. My Mum used to say I had legs like bananas because they were so bandy!

It's amazing to think that I was ever that small. Yet there I am, frozen in time. I can remember how all the grown ups seemed like giants. I couldn't reach door handles so Mum and Dad would have to open the door for me. Mum would bath me and feed me and take me out. If I lost her in the shops, I'd cry because I thought I might never see her again.

I was about six here. Just started school. I look quite pretty, don't I? That was our uniform — green with a white shirt and grey skirt. I've got really pale skin and huge black eyes. Babyface.

Mum took me to school on my first day. I was so excited. Mum said school was a nice place and I would learn my ABC and how to read books and do sums.

I loved school. I liked my teacher. The first book I ever read was *The Gingerbread Man*.

> I love to read. I read lots of books. I sit in the big chair in the kitchen while Mummy cooks dinner and she listens to me.
> 'No, you don't say that word like that. You say it like this.'
> 'Mummy what does this word mean?'
> 'Can you spell it for me angel?'
> 'It's got a "k" and a "n" and a "o" and a "w"...'
> I didn't know lots of words before I went to school. Now I can

1 My self in echoes

read. I'm so proud. I know lots of words. My teacher is proud of me. She puts lots of ticks in my books.

It must have been around this time. This must have been when it started.

You know, I have watched the faces of children at play. So small. Their necks tilting right back when they look up at you. Small hands on your calf to help them balance. Eyes huge with wonderment. Always enquiring — not seeing the evil in the world because they haven't learnt about that yet. Responding to a smile with a smile.

Unaffected laughter. They believe what you tell them. Why shouldn't they?

And I see myself as I was then. I see *my* face in the faces of the innocent. I must have seen things as they do.
Once. Perhaps.
I look at photos of myself when I was a child and I strain to see traces of my past.
Nothing is betrayed.
My smile is the standard school photo grin. 'Say cheese please.'
I look at myself and think 'How could he?'
I look at children and think how *small* they are.
How *trusting* they are.
How *defenceless*.
And that was *me*.

> I hear the blood beating in my ears. My eyes feel all puffy. I can't see. It's dark. I am snuggled under my covers. I am in *my* bed. I know I am.
> I am in *my* room. I know I am.
> There is a sickly smell. The air is being crushed out of my body. A giant. It's the Nightmonster.
> He's trying to kill me. I can't breathe. There is something hard and sharp. Pain. Want to cry. Can't get my breath to cry.
> Out of the blackness there is a voice. It's Daddy's voice. He says, 'Be quiet.' He says, 'Don't tell Mummy.' The pain goes on and on. Big hands. Daddy's hot breath stealing my air from me. I want to be a good girl. So I won't cry. Not until Daddy has gone and he can't hear me.

At school there was a big emphasis on safety. I suppose there is in lots of schools. You know the kind of thing, 'Don't play with matches,' 'Learn to swim.' There were two big campaigns when I was in the infants, to teach children how to cross roads properly. We lived in quite a busy area and there were frequent road accidents. We were also taught not to go with strangers. We had a film and a colouring book to fill in. A local police officer came in to talk to us about it.

Don't play with matches.
Don't run across roads.
Don't go with strangers.
They became a mantra for lots of children.
We all realised the seriousness of what adults were telling us.
Well, I never did any of those things. I was a good girl.
I did *exactly* what my parents told me to do.
Like all good children do.
Like all good children, I was kept in ignorance.
You can't protect yourself from what you're not aware of.
And no-one knew that better than my Dad.

This is a picture of him and me together. It's the only one I keep of us. I try to remember that he must have been young once too. And that he probably knew exactly how it felt to be an abused child.
This one was taken on the prom near home. I can't have been more than seven years old there. Still got those bandy legs! I look quite cheerful there.
You'd never be able to tell would you? Not just by looking. I think that's what freaks so many people out.
He doesn't *look* like a 'pervert'. He's not wearing a dirty old raincoat. He looks... normal. Respectable.
And a lot of people did respect him. Especially from our community. It's not easy for a black man to build himself up from nothing. Become a self made man. Not in this country.

>'What's *your* name then?'
>'Khadija.'
>'Where are you from?'
>'Round the corner, Penny Lane.'
>'No you're not. I know you. Your dad's a Paki.
>That means you're a Paki too.'

Yeah I did tell Mum about it. I was seven.

>'Don't tell.'
>'No, Daddy.'

I *always* knew it was wrong. Because I *felt* it was wrong. I had 'no' feelings about it. I told Mum because I wanted it to stop but I had no idea that he would react in the way that he did.

1 My self in echoes

> I love my Mummy. She makes me feel happy. She reads me stories. She plays snap with me and combs my hair and cuddles me.
> One day I tell her about the Nightmonster. It hurts when I do a wee so I tell her that Daddy hugs me very hard and it hurts and I don't like it. I don't know big words.
> I'm sore.
> I don't know the right words.
> I ask her to ask Daddy to stop. She's a grown up. She *can* ask him. She's a grown up. He will listen.
> Mummy asks Daddy about it. But Daddy says it was just a pretend game. Then, he gets angry. He shouts for me and I have to stand in front of him. He shouts and shouts and I must not move because he'll get me anyway.

I remember I could only see up to his knees...

> ...I don't want to see his face, because I know it's gone all horrible and his eyes have gone all big and starey. I don't know what I've done wrong...

...I did not understand what I had done wrong...

> ...the first hit makes me fall down. He is shouting and his big hands are hitting me.
> He hits Mummy too.
> I spoke.
> I broke the law. I spoke.
> That's why...

...The Law of Silence was beaten into me.
I never needed to be taught it again.

I don't remember the minutes after that. I think I must have cried after he left. Nobody spoke about it again. No photographs of *that*! Only the ones left in my head.

Mum thought I had forgotten about it but I never did.
I have always remembered.

The days after that must have gone on the same. Mum would wake me in the mornings. Make my breakfast and take me to school. Then, she would work all day. Even when I came home from school she would have to go back to work.
And my Dad too.
Then, I would have my dinner and go to bed and sleep.
But only if the Nightmonster didn't come and wake me up.

> *'Don't ever tell again. I'll kill you if you do.'*
> *'No, Daddy.'*
> And in the dark, the Nightmonster came out of the shadows. He sticks his horrible tongue in my mouth. Then, there is the pain. He makes funny noises and breathes all funny.
> He takes away my air.

When I was nine, I remember I read a book. I wanted to be a doctor when I grew up. So I liked to read books about the body. This book had a section in it about 'Human Reproduction'. I felt so upset when I had read it. I knew now that my Dad's 'private parts' could make me have a baby. I felt sick.
It was also obvious that only 'grown ups' were supposed to do that kind of thing. Mums and Dads. Not Dads and their little girls. I felt ill. Ill in my stomach.
But I couldn't tell Mum because I wasn't allowed to. I couldn't break the Law of Silence.
I couldn't let *anybody* know ever. I would die with the secret inside me.
I began to invent ways of killing any child that might be inside me. I would kill it by not eating.
I would hurt my stomach so it couldn't live.
I didn't know about periods then. I didn't know I couldn't conceive.
I grew quieter. Mum called me 'mouse' because I was so quiet.

> *'Mouse..Mousie...Is anything wrong Mouse? Has anybody upset you?'*
> *'No, Mummy.'*
> *'Yes. But I'm not allowed to tell you.'*

In the school playground, I was the only one who played alone. I didn't get on with children of my age. I knew I was different. I was different in lots of ways. But I didn't feel superior.
I felt inferior.
Different race. My name sounded funny, they had said. Khadija. Half of them couldn't even pronounce it.
Different religion. I didn't join in prayers or hymns about Jesus. Nobody tried to understand me. I prayed at home. In Arabic. My Dad saw to it that his children would be good Muslims.

> *'Honour thy father and thy mother.'*
> *'Honour thy father...'*
> God will punish me. God will send me to Hell.
> This is adultery. This is wrong.

1 My self in echoes

This was taken when I was eleven. I was quite podgy then. Puppy fat, Mum said.
I started secondary school. That's why the uniform is different. Blue shirt, jumper and skirt.
Mum has collected so many school photos of me.
She even bought the horrendous ones — like when I blinked just as the flash went off, or when I was covered in spots! Some things don't change, eh?

I thought a new school would mean a new start. I thought the abuse would end, but instead it got much worse.
I started my periods. My Dad had just assaulted me. It was a hot sunny, Sunday morning. I felt sticky and ill. I went to the toilet and found myself covered in blood.
I thought my Dad had damaged my insides. I told Mum and she said, 'Don't worry. It's just your first period.'
I felt a sense of dread engulf me.
From now on the thing that I feared most of all could happen. I could get pregnant.

School was the only escape that I had now. I worked really hard and was in the top sets for most subjects. I was the model pupil. Compliant, attentive, quiet.
I was painfully shy. Nobody thought my behaviour strange because my behaviour was completely acceptable.
I was a good girl.

> 'Well done, Khadija. Another excellent report. Lots of grade A*s*. Keep up the good work!'

Well done, Yeah, I worked hard. I worked hard to forget.

> '— And you don't mess around with boys. They're dirty. Boys only want one thing. You stay away from them.
> When the times comes, I will arrange a marriage for you to a good Muslim boy.'
> '— Yes, Dad.'

I felt dirty and guilty. You can't imagine how I felt. I felt like the lowest, filthiest thing alive. No amount of water and soap could ever get me clean, because I was rotten on the inside.
I was petrified that everyone could see what I was.
Afraid that if I spoke I might give myself away.
Who wanted to listen to me anyway?
I was worthless. I was nothing.
My grade 'A' reports were worthless pieces of paper. They were not

enough to purify me. Reprieve me. I was damned. I would burn in Hell.

I didn't know what incest was until I was thirteen. I read about it in a woman's magazine that my Mum had bought. It wasn't a main feature. It was a tiny article spread just above an advert for convenience foods or something mundane like that. But this wasn't mundane.
It told me what I already knew.
Incest was wrong. It also had a name. It existed.

I remember my hands shaking as I was reading the article and how they shook as I ripped out the article and tore it into thousands of little pieces.
I was sickened. Appalled.

This was a state of mind that never left me. I was tormented by what I was.
There was something wrong with me.
I was to blame in some way.
I must be. I withdrew into my own, personal Hell.

> In my head, Mum, In my head is the only time I can tell you. And you can't hear my thoughts. It's a good job. He'll kill me if I tell you.
> He keeps me away from you. I can't reach you. I'm afraid.
> Something really bad is happening to me and I think it's my fault. I just want it to stop.
> I don't want him to go to prison.
> I don't want to go into care. I want it to stop and we can be like a proper family.

I couldn't tell her because Dad kept us apart. We weren't allowed to go shopping together — I wasn't allowed out after school, you see. We weren't allowed to enjoy each other's company. If he saw us happy together, there was trouble. I would be picked on. So would Mum.
The atmosphere at home was terrible when he was there. We were all isolated from each other.

An uncle of mine came to stay. Only for a few days. He seemed okay, you know? I didn't really trust him because he was a man but I thought...I don't know what I thought. How can it be that a child isn't safe in her own home?

I was sitting reading. He was in the room. I don't want to go into details, but I was just reading.
I was so shocked. I didn't fight him. I hadn't been taught to fight. I

1 My self in echoes

didn't say, 'No.' I hadn't been taught *how* to say 'No.'

Afterwards, I just stood for a while, motionless, whilst he grinned at me and asked me 'had I liked it?' I couldn't speak properly. I said I had to go to the toilet and I left the room. I went to my room and burst into tears. I felt like a whore. What was wrong with me to make two men do this to me?
I was evil and rotten and *he'd seen what I was.*

My mum came back home. I told her. It was like having a piece of me ripped out. Some invisible hand had hold of my intestines and was pulling them out of me through my mouth.
She looked very pale. She told Dad.

Dad was dead concerned. Indignant. He asked what had happened and I told him through tears. He didn't blame me at all but threw my uncle out of the house. My uncle claimed that it was just an affectionate joke. I was too stunned to feel anything then.
Now, I am outraged.

I had thought that things might now change for me. Hope is a strange thing. People put up with terrible things because they believe things will change by some miracle of human nature...

> Dad has seen how upset I am about uncle. Maybe he sees that I'm upset about what he is doing too. Maybe it will all end now, after all this time?

...No. Next day everything was back to normal.
I've learnt now. If you want change, then you have to be responsible for it yourself. You can't rely on the hope of change in the man who is sexually abusing you, even if he is your Dad.

The abuse became worse. More frequent. I hated myself for not having told Mum about what Dad was doing as well as what my uncle had done. Why? Why had I missed my chance for freedom? I understand now of course, that telling about Dad had more serious consequences, but at that time my reasoning told me that I hadn't told because I was a stupid bitch who enjoyed it. Otherwise, why would I not tell?

That's a photo of me when I was fifteen. I look tired but other than that, it's the same old school photo smile. Longer hair. Thinner, but no change outwardly.

Things at home were much, much worse. I think my Dad was falling to pieces — disintegrating. Just as I was. He had become more violent — against me — but more so against the rest of the family. It was a way of ensuring my compliance. If I didn't do exactly what I was told to, then they would suffer too.

When he flew into a mood, it was terrifying. Have you ever been in a situation where you had nowhere to run? Have you ever been forced to submit to violence?
Try and imagine what it's like. Just try. To be beaten up and raped in your own home by your own father.
Try and imagine what it's like watching the people you love being beaten too, knowing that if you intervene the hands will turn on you. I once watched him beat up my Mum when she was eight months pregnant. I thought he was going to kill her.

So you see, I felt that I was not just responsible for myself.
It was up to me to keep them safe.

Dad was more vigilant about me. I think he had become afraid, more than ever, that I would tell. Incest was creeping out of the woodwork — programmes on T.V. had just begun to dare to tell the stories of people like me.
He even watched one with Mum and me. He commented on how awful it was. Like a Janus, another face always ready to hide what he was doing. His respectability was the permanent greasepaint he wore. He fooled everybody. My Mum, his family, her family, my teachers, his friends.
None of them were stupid. *You* probably would have been fooled too if you had met him.
Frightening, isn't it?
Life would be so much easier if all sex offenders wore dirty raincoats. Don't you think so?

> i am no longer, I.
> If i look depressed He will hit me.
> He will slap my face like He did this morning.
> Doesn't He know why i am depressed?
> He wants me to be His puppet. i am his clown.
> i am not allowed to have any emotion.
>
> Ten past four. Oh God. Ten past four.
> Dad will be in.
> If i can just slide the key slowly, the door won't make a noise.
> Slowly. No noise.
> He has heard me.
> He hears every time.
>
> He will be lying in bed. All crumpled sheets around Him. The

1 My self in echoes

room will smell of tobacco and *Him*. That smell has travelled with me since i can remember.

i could kill him. i could get Him with his scissors while He's asleep. But what if He opens His eyes? i won't be able to do it if He opens His eyes. And He's much stronger than me.
And He knows Karate. He would kill me.

i will lie next to Him. i will start it off as He has taught me to.
i know every move inside out. i am involved against my will.
i am bought with money.
i am made to say i enjoy it.
i will leave revolted.
i will wash off the stains that He leaves on me.
i am infected.
He is inside me. In every pore.

But i am Khadija. i'm a good girl. i get grade *A*s.
i pray like good Muslim girls do.

i am a whore. i am dirty. i am nothing.
i am buried alive, in a coffin of silence.

Other times my Dad would talk to me and twist the knots already in my head. He would cry like a child.
The Nightmonster would sob.
And I would sit. Like a fool, I was moved by him.
I only wanted it to stop. That's all I wanted.
In my dreams, it would end and he would be a normal Dad. But it was always next week, next month. Next year. And I was becoming invisible. I decided that I'd kill myself. It was the only way out.
I tried to go through with it on more occasions than I can remember. But fear or hope always drove me back.
I'm sorry. I need another coffee. Do you want one?

A cousin of mine came to stay. This is her, wearing her Shalwar and Kameez. It's a traditional dress. She came from Bangladesh to visit. It's really because of her that I told, and because of the Horizon programme on incest.
She told me how uncomfortable she was feeling.
You see, Dad started to say things to her. Odd things. Things an uncle doesn't say.
But things an abuser does.
They were the same things he said to me.

I resolved to tell Mum about it. After plucking up courage, I decided to do it. She was washing curtains at the time. When I'd told her what Dad had said to my cousin, Mum looked shocked. I was sweating. Thoughts running through my head. I was sweating and looking at my feet. A million voices in my head, telling me, 'Tell! Tell *now*!'

My breath failed me and I could hardly hear myself speaking over the thudding of my heart. I spoke. I said the words. I broke the Law.

The silence that followed terrified me.

Would she call me a liar?

Would she believe me?

My Mum's face had never looked so pale and drawn. It looked like wax.

And then her arms were cradling me, just as they had done when I was small.

She spoke to me.

'How long?'

'I told you once when I was little...'

She looked devastated. I just felt numb.

When we had 'recovered', we phoned an incest helpline and they advised us on what we could do. Mum decided to pack Dad's bags. She did it mechanically, with dry eyed compulsion. Too shocked even to cry.

My cousin was upset. She was blaming me for everything.

I ignored her as best I could.

And we waited for Dad to come home.

The front door slammed at about half past six. And he was home. We were all sitting in the front room waiting for him to make an appearance. And then he was in the room, looking relaxed, a little tired.

He'd been working hard.

He instantly knew something was wrong. Mum sat looking at him like a pillar of stone. I don't know what must have been running through her head.

> I met you and I loved you. I gave up my religion for you. I married you in the face of hatred and ostracism *because I loved you*. We worked hard for what we have. I worked harder. We have been together for twenty two years and married seventeen of them. I have given up my name to carry yours, and be a part of you. I have fought to understand you, even when you have treated me like nothing. I have had children by you and raised them, loved them and cared for them. And all this time, all this time, I have never known you at all. — Even though I have

1 My self in echoes

shared your thoughts, your bed, your life. You are a stranger. I am contaminated.
You have betrayed me. I have been blind...

'I know.' That was all he said.
My Dad was thrown but not completely. The lines he had rehearsed for so long were no longer appropriate to the context. My Mum started to rip into him with her confrontation. He had to improvise. All innocence, he seemed repulsed, horrified by what he was being accused of.
'Father and daughter?' he kept repeating. 'What do you think I am?'
I sat absolutely terrified. I can remember having pins and needles in my legs. I thought I was going to wet myself. I was convinced that I was going to die. I was going to be murdered and that was going to be the end of me. He was going to kill us all.
And then I was terrified that it was all going to happen again — that he would convince her that it was all pretend, I'd made it up. I wanted to speak, to defend myself but I couldn't open my mouth.

'Come upstairs.' Oh God. He's talking to me. 'I want to talk to you.'
'You stay close to me, Khadj. I'm telling *you* to go. Your bags are packed. I want you out of the house. If you don't go, I'm phoning the police.'
Oh no. Don't want her to phone the police. i just want it to stop. i don't want any trouble *please*. i'll go into care or He'll go to prison, if there's trouble.

He didn't budge in his denial. So my Mum got up and phoned the police. I couldn't believe it. It was the last thing I wanted to happen. But looking back, I think it was necessary — there was no telling what he might have done otherwise. He was a violent man.
After she came back from the phone, he was just standing, not knowing what to do. He tried to go over to the police station and tell them it had been a false alarm. But it was too late. The call had gone through to another station.
By the time he came back to the house, they were already waiting for him.
Tall people in black and white uniforms had invaded our home. He burst into tears. It had all been a terrible mistake, officer. He was a respectable man.
Then he got angry.
His parting shot to Mum was 'Make sure you get your daughter examined.'
And so ended seventeen years of marriage.

After he was taken away, so were we. I was frightened that the neighbours might see us being bundled into the car with its flashing blue lights. How would I explain it, if they had? I wasn't really aware of what was going on. Nobody had told me. I wasn't really there, just as I never was when things were too much for me. I was frozen in my silence.
I just stared into the space in front of me, as we were driven to the police station.

This was a nightmare. It wasn't real. I felt like I was having one of those nightmares when you're walking down an endless dark corridor and your legs are moving but you aren't getting anywhere. It seemed like that in the police station. Disembodied faces drifted past me.

I was forced to wake up when I reached the interview room. I *wish* I had a photo of that to show you. It was awful. The lights were so bright, they hurt my eyes and it was really clinical. There were filing cabinets and a huge desk.
We sat on one side of this desk, me and Mum, placed on hard chairs. On the other side, a male officer sat, poised to ask the details.

My little sister ran amok around the room. She seemed to find the litter bin absolutely fascinating — but then, that's what children are like. I watched her and then looked around the room to avoid looking at the man sitting opposite me. My eyes landed on a soft porn calender, dangling from the wall; the empty eyes looked at me, her body contorted into an inviting position. I felt sick. Ill and embarrassed. That was what they would think I had been.

A woman took notes. She smiled at me. She had a kind face but it was a He who asked the questions. And it's no good saying 'thing' if you mean 'penis', okay? You have to say it.

After the initial interview, I was driven to another station for a medical. It was late at night now. I didn't want a medical at all. But I had no choice. Well, there was nothing new there, was there? Except this was all legal of course.

I wanted to go into the examination without Mum because I couldn't bear her to see me like that. The room was like a doctor's surgery with cabinets filled with lots of brightly coloured bottles.
The surgeon was a man, a He.

The woman PC stayed with me. Tried to cheer me up even. I was really glad that she was there. I never saw her again, but I've wanted to say 'thank you' to her for a long time. She helped me while I took my clothes off.

1 My self in echoes

I felt really humiliated. I just feel that it was another abuse to be interviewed by a man, and then to be examined by another man.

> He is getting out rubber gloves, and bags and a torch and long swabs, What's he going to *do* to me?
> 'Can you open your legs...'
> 'Is it hurting? It'll be over soon. You're making it worse for yourself. You should try and relax...'
> 'Oh, he's been in there all right...'
> I *know* he has. I *told* you he has. I wasn't fantasising you know.
> 'You can put your clothes back on now. You'll be interviewed again tomorrow. The worst of this is over now.'
> Oh.

I didn't sleep well that night, as you can imagine. The next day, I was taken to the station again with my Mum. It was daytime and everything looked different in the light. The room we sat in was horrible and dingy. It looked like an old store room! It did, honest! It was really seedy. I was interviewed by a woman, and she was sympathetic towards me. But even so, the whole thing was terrible to me.
I'd spent so long trying to forget it all. Trying to cope and carry on, and I'd done it because I'd detached myself from what was happening to me.
My Mum looked really sick and haggard. She was there because I needed support. I needed someone to hold my hand. And I wanted her to know. I wanted her to know it all.
She sat with me for five hours while I vomited up the details of my abuse.
What? When? How often? What did he do? What did you do? Did he come? Why didn't you tell?
And I had to answer using the words I hated.
Well, it's no good saying 'thing' if you mean 'penis', okay? You have to say it.
And finally, I was allowed to leave. They had my statement all signed and checked. My underwear was in a plastic bag in some forensics lab. And they had poked around my body to see if there was evidence of abuse. It wasn't enough to get him all that he was guilty of though. Insufficient medical evidence.
He admitted to a lesser charge. I don't want to say what it was. The whole thing still sickens me.

He got a year prison sentence. Six months with remission. I'm told that I am lucky that he got that much. I know it's true. I've met a lot of victims who took it to court and watched their abusers walk free.

I still feel that justice wasn't done though. He received no therapy. He's started a new family now. Remarried; I've got a little half brother somewhere.
God help him.

And what about me? If you look back at my photos, you'll see the ones of me with other girls. Well, they're from the Girls' Group I joined a few weeks later. All of us in that photo had been victims. I really needed those Groups. It gave me a chance to meet other victims, and share my feelings, without having to explain the graphics of what had happened to me.

I was really low at that time too. I had to wait a year for the case to go to court, in which time my Dad was out on bail. That meant, I often saw him in the street, or driving around in his car. Although there was an injunction against him seeing us, I was convinced he was going to come and get me in the night. He'd kill us all.
I needed a release from that tension, and this is how I got it.

That's the day we went to a fair at New Brighton just outside Liverpool. It was really hot and sunny. I had such a laugh. We were all messing around, going on all the rides. I was being a child again. And nobody told me off. Nobody told any of us off. This photo is of Sue, Rachel, Liz and me on the Waltzers. Sue was the youngest — she was only eleven when that was taken. Liz was thirteen. I think Rachel was sixteen and I was fifteen and a half.

This is one where one of the women who ran the group, Trish, made us all line up on the prom to have our photo taken. That's why I'm pulling such a face — *hated* being photographed. That's Anne who ran the group too. I think we must have had her tormented sometimes; she is one of my best friends now. I don't know what any of the girls in the photo are up to now. There's one girl, Michelle, who isn't in the photograph, who I still keep in touch with.
We were the 'baggy jumper and jeans' twins of the group. We never used to wear anything else.
Well, I guess miracles *can* happen! I've even been known to wear the odd t-shirt or even *a dress* since then!

These are photographs of my family over that summer. We went out a lot, now that we could.
That's a lovely park near our home that's got a lake and Japanese gardens. We all used to just go and sit there, eating ice cream and taking in the perfume and colours of the flowers.

Things were really tense at home then, because of the court case. My Mum had to come to terms with her own pain at what had happened. She had to reassess herself as a woman and as a mother. She felt

1 My self in echoes

terrible that I had never told her what was going on for the eight years, after I first told when I was seven.
She was sickened that she hadn't heard me when I was little. But how could she have done? Incest wasn't talked about. It didn't happen. She had married a respected man who wouldn't *do* that kind of thing.

I felt really mad at her, at myself and the world in general.
Why hadn't somebody seen what was happening to me?
Why hadn't I been believed when I was seven?
Why hadn't I told for so long?
Like someone who has been suffocated for years and then is suddenly allowed to breathe, the sudden rush of air to my lungs was almost too much to bear. It was something I could be swept away by. Something I couldn't control. The uncertainty and self doubt that freedom brought with it was not something I had expected.

Depression followed. It sat inside me for many months. I tried hard to fight it and carry on, but finally, after the prescriptions of brightly coloured anti depressants had done nothing to kill my pain, I came off them and for the first time in my life I grieved for my lost belongings.

Mum and me directed a lot of our hurt at each other. We had to work hard to become a mother and daughter again. But eventually the awful slanging matches subsided and I believe we have found the peace that we deserve, in each other.
She is my inspiration because she believed me, stood by me and has supported me in all that I have done since — within reason of course!

It makes me so angry when people judge situations so quickly. They form their beliefs so readily on false assumptions and incomplete knowledge. Neither Mum nor I, were to blame for what happened. We have both struggled hard to gain that knowledge. We have both reached a higher level of understanding.
So neither of us should be labelled and patronized. Neither of us will be.
I don't want pity. I'm too outraged to be pitied. Anger is a powerful weapon and I have used it to fight back. To *make* people listen. Because now that I know I have a voice, I intend to use it.

i have finally become I. I am able to say that I am proud that I have survived my abuse. I am proud to have the mother I have. I am proud to call myself mixed race, when, for so long any acknowledgement of my racial background, meant an acknowledgement of my Dad. And I wanted him purged out of every pore.
But now I realise that incest and the sexual abuse of children occurs everywhere. In every class, in every society regardless of religion or

colour or status, you will find male and female victims of abuse. Victims, unfortunately, are everywhere. So too, fortunately, are Survivors.

See these? These are pictures of me on matriculation day when I got into university. These are my mates here. That was taken last year. I'm in my second year now. I like to think sometimes, of how pissed off it would make Dad feel if he knew that I'd managed to get 4 grade 'As' and a 'B' at A level, as well as two S levels. It'd be even better if he knew that I'd got a place at Oxford.
He hasn't beaten me.

I am an adult now. I am the same age that my Mum was when she was married, and pregnant with me.
I am a 'grown-up'. *I* am a thing that children stand in awe of.
I can still see my face as it must have been, in *their* faces.
And I am horrified.
We keep children in ignorance.
We warn them about strangers. Not about friends, family or professionals.

Now after the rude awakening of Cleveland, we know children can be sexually abused, but only *other* people's children. Not *our* children.
And if *our* children say that they are being sexually abused then it's lies, or a mistake or we'll just ignore it or the doctor made the wrong diagnosis or the mum was to blame. Anything, *anything* but the truth.

That's why I *have* to tell my story. And other Survivors should do the same. I have only come as far as I have because so many people have cared. They have helped me. They have believed me.
I know plenty of victims who have been made to suffer as much in telling, as they did in abuse.
And it disgusts me.
That's why I am doing your chapter. And I'll keep writing until 'grown-ups' start listening to the truth, and start making their children aware; believing and helping those who have been abused. Until people start putting children first.

Part 1
Children in society

2 Children in society
Penelope Leach

The first time I had to address a children's organisation the topic was 'Infant separation and stranger anxiety' and I spoke to parents and workers in one hall while their babies and toddlers cried for them in the one next door. The irony struck nobody but me and it was another year before I first found the courage to say 'Wouldn't we all be happier if they joined us?' But that only worked once. When I was invited back three years later the organisers told me kindly that they had sited the creche in a different part of the building, 'because we know it bothers you to hear them cry...' What really bothers me is that it does not bother everybody, but nowadays I am often told reproachfully: 'Today is for the parents; they don't want to have to think about their children.'

There are millions of individuals who are no more capable than I of tuning-out children's expressions of distress. There are many groups of people — some of them represented in this book — who devote their professional lives to children, and are praised (if seldom highly paid) for doing so. Countless words each year are written and spoken about children's needs and few recent issues have attracted more attention from the media than child abuse. But, sadly, I believe that this tide of concern for children is more apparent than real and often more anti-parent than pro-child. If there is such an entity as 'society', this one is indifferent to children as individuals and

2 Children in society

therefore has no special interest in the people who are their parents. Only headlined tragedy breaks through that indifference and then children, as a category, become objects of a social concern that usually manages to pin-point their parents as blameworthy.

If this is so, all of us who work for children as people are swimming against the social tide. No wonder the tiny islands of child-centred excellence some people work so hard to create seldom coalesce into viable land-masses on which we can build a more child-friendly environment.

That social tide is undercutting the relationships and lifestyles on which all personal caring roles, including parenting, depend. Post-industrial Britain has become a society of individualistic work-place based adults, for whom money is the arbiter of value and means of exchange rather than a symbol of value and means to our ends. Few people today can work for a living in the sense of choosing where and how they will live and then working as much — and only as much — as they need work to support that lifestyle. Even fewer have, or expect to have, personal motivation for work other than the accumulation of money and goods for their own sake and for the sake of the social status and associated self-image they attract. Satisfaction in the actual processes of daily work, or in anything it produces other than money, is a rare privilege and so is the time and energy to enjoy what that money buys. It is not only the workaholic executive who lives to work; it is all of us who applaud a reduction in basic weekly working hours, knowing that the difference will not be more non-working hours for living, but more money from overtime. It is as if society itself has forgotten what economic productivity is for: forgotten that there is more to a viable and beneficient society than per capita income or the balance of trade....

With production as god and the market as a place of worship, anything that cannot be directly bought with money and sold for profit is of peripheral interest; non-productive people, such as the elderly, the chronically ill and all those with special needs, are marginalised and limited resources are allocated according to cost benefit analysis. Only on this basis could expenditure on major heart surgery to enable a few earners to keep on working be seen as a better investment than the chiropody that would keep millions of older people comfortably mobile.

Children are a special case. No cost-benefit analysis is needed to prove that they are any society's most vital investment. They are the producer/consumer units of the future; the aging population is an economist's nightmare and the coming shortage of school-leavers is keeping many an industrialist awake at night. But it takes a long time for an investment in children to produce a return and in the interim of childhood they are doubly non-productive. They do not only cost money they cannot earn for themselves, they also absorb adult time that could otherwise be spent in productive work. How fortunate that those babies and children that society must have, but cannot really use until they grow up, are part of personal fulfilment for many of its members who will therefore accept the sacrifices involved in supporting them.

Children as possessions — and millstones

Babies and young children are often regarded as personal possessions or extensions of their parents rather than as members of society in their own right. The message seems to be: 'It's natural that people should want to have children. OK. Go ahead. But any children you have are your responsibility, added on to your existing responsibilities as producers and consumers. So don't expect any special privileges because you are also parents.' It sounds reasonable; it is widely accepted by past parents who reared their children in a different society, and by future parents who cannot see what they are getting into. But it is the trap in which today's parents are struggling.

The trap is ludicrously simple. Babies and young children need to be cared for by familiar adults in suitable places twenty-four hours a day. Society expects all able-bodied citizens of working age to earn the money they need at specialised jobs that cannot combine with childcare, in specialised places that are not suitable for children. People cannot be in two places at once, ergo there is no obvious or easy way for most individuals to be simultaneously solvent good citizens and good parents.

Personal care for dependent individuals including children was (and in many parts of the world still is) met within diverse extended family groups where it can be flexibly shared amongst many people as best suits the immediate work commitments of each. That is a rare model for here and now. Our families have been small for several generations so there are few extensive kin-networks. Where they exist they are often geographically dispersed. And where they exist in a single community, all the adults, of both generations, are similarly committed to the marketplace so that outside rural communities, grandmothers can seldom be counted on for childcare. Although we still regard a 'nuclear family' as the 'normal' household for a child to be born into, it is often unclear what it is the nucleus of, or what relationships constitute 'family'. By no means all start out with two acknowledged parents, let alone partners in legal marriage; less than two thirds of married parents remain together until their youngest child leaves school and many 'broken homes' re-form, once or several times, bringing in different parent-figures and perhaps half of step-siblings. Today's most widely extended 'families' usually result from multiple partnerships but seldom result in a network of care for children.

If the people who are likely to be 'at home' have changed, so has the nature and function of home itself, especially in its almost complete separation from productive activity. Home is no longer the centre of most peoples' lives; for many it is little more than a place for rest and recreation after work and a shower and clean clothes before it. Work belongs to geographically separate, hi-tech mass-production or distribution units where tasks are too specialised for flexible sharing and no child would be safe or happy for long even if s/he were welcome. So children have lost their taken-for-granted presence in, and eventual apprenticeship to, productive adult work and a range of adult people. They are confined to sharing the small and interim part of their parents' lives that is home. And there, where people who are not parenting do not work but rest from work, the work that children themselves require is highlighted as disruptive.

These modern conundrums of childcare are shared by most highly developed economies, but the UK and North America are unique in their refusal to face them and facilitate the search for solutions.

Our society could honestly admit what sections of it still sometimes appear to believe: 'Parents cannot care for their babies and work, so mothers should usually stay at home and fathers should go out and earn for the family,' and set male wages and salaries accordingly, as in Japan.

Or it could say 'Parents cannot care for their babies during working hours so that is our job,' and produce a network of free daycare for all, as in China.

Or it could say 'Parents cannot care for their babies during working hours so they must not be economically penalised if they do not work while their children are young,' and produce universal financial support for either parent to be at home, or divide his or her time flexibly between work and home, as in Sweden.

Or it could say 'The early rearing of a child *is* productive work, at least as important an investment for society as postgraduate education or specialised training,' and arrange for high-status, grant-aided, collegiate-type childcare breaks for either parent, as many of us would wish.

But our society will say nothing that acknowledges that children legitimately alter peoples' lives and do nothing that involves public expenditure on private families. It will not risk the political dynamite or wage inflation of open support for a sexist division of labour. It will not make daycare universally available because children are their parents' responsibility, not the responsibility of the State. Its lukewarm support for workplace nurseries suggests that if industry needs mothers, industry should tempt them back with childcare 'perks' equated with other perks like luncheon vouchers. It thus acknowledges the increasing importance of women as workers without admitting to their importance as mothers or to the importance of their children. It will not seriously consider adequate financial support for a parent who chooses to be at home because people in this society are only paid for economically productive work and caring for your own children is not seen as such. And it will certainly not recognise parenting as a special, and especially valuable, segment of some adult working lives because it does not truly recognise meeting the needs of children as a good investment.

Children in poverty

So people are left to struggle with the parent/worker dilemma, and the one thing they can be certain of is social censure when they fail on either count. And some degree of 'failure' is unavoidable for a rising proportion of parents, especially mothers.

The last decade has seen a widening of the gulf between rich and middle-income and between middle-income and poor. In 1985, 5 million people (just over 9% of the population) were living on less than half the country's average income. By 1987 that figure had risen by half again, to 7.7 million people (over 14% of the population). Women and their children were inevitably targeted for a disproportionate share in that increasing relative poverty. As we went into the nineties, there were over one million single-parent families with 1.6 million children in Britain. Most single parents are women and two thirds of them were poor enough to claim income support. There were 2.6 million women in full-time, and 3.4 million in part-time paid work, who earned less than the European Decency Threshold of £148 per week. On those calculations employed women made up two thirds of the low paid. Figures for unemployed married women with children are hard to calculate because many see no point in registering for employment that lack of childcare facilities would prevent them taking up and those who do register do not count as 'unemployed' if their husbands have jobs, even though nobody pays them for the work they do. Although such women work at home and are not paid, they have to pay poll tax. At least as originally imposed, that tax directly increased the financial cost to a family of sacrificing one income to children's care, and further increased the economic dependence of these 'non-working women' on their male partners. Child benefit, the only income available to all mothers as a right, remained frozen at less than half the official sum added to supplementary benefit for a child aged eleven to fourteen. According to the government's own figures, published in July 1990, by 1987 more than one in five of the nation's children were living in families receiving less than half average income.

Self-reliance and enterprise were the new watchwords of the eighties; getting rid of dependency the moral justification for 'reform' of State benefits. But during the early years of childcare, the time, energy and flexibility required for 'enterprise' are scarce, and self-reliance takes on a new meaning when that self must also be relied upon by small children. So, many policies intended to help people towards a higher standard of living, with greater dignity and personal choice, have increased the relative disadvantage of young families. The ideal of a property-owning democracy, for example, was the justification for the withdrawal of housing subsidy and rate support grants from local authorities and the consequent rise in rent and rates, mitigated only by means-tested housing benefit. While some (usually older and/or better-off) people who had expected to be council tenants all their lives now own their own homes, the resulting housing-situation is increasingly desperate for those who must compete for a dwindling pool of less and less subsidised local authority rentals, or for housing association and privately rented accommodation with little security of tenure or rent-control. According to a recent Policy Studies Institute survey (March 1990), 5% of households — over 1 million families — are in serious rent arrears and a similar number are in trouble with mortgage repayments. The birth of a baby is a leading cause of this indebtedness, alongside redundancy and partnership breakdown, and almost half of all single parents have at least one serious debt. How much real choice about going out to a paid job does a mother have if not doing so means that neither she nor her children will have a home to stay in? Yet how can she go if there is no-one to care for her child?

One way or another more and more families are becoming homeless. Official figures reported 7,652 in 1970, 56,750 in 1979 and 128,350 in 1988. 1990 figures will undoubtedly show an even steeper rise. If adolescents sleeping rough are the most obvious evidence — the shame that caught Mother Theresa's eye on her visit to London from Calcutta — the thousands of babies and small children crammed into bed-and-breakfast accommodation (more than 12,000 in London alone) are a hidden and horrible indictment of us all.

Once a family with young children begins to be waterlogged by poverty, the weight increases until it is impossible to shake it off and climb to dry ground and a new launch. The children's need for continual care limits parents' freedom to work, travel in search of work or even seek help from distant, overcrowded agencies. Their continual growth and development demands replacement of items such as clothes and shoes that wreck tight weekly budgets, and one-off purchases — cots, pushchairs, bedding, toys — that such a budget simply cannot meet. Cumulative deprivations sink the family further and further below a normal lifestyle. Discretionary grants — never lavish or easy to obtain — used sometimes to serve as lifebelts, ensuring that a parent (especially one who was in touch with a good health visitor or social worker) could buy items, such as a safety-approved fireguard, that kept her being, and feeling, adequate as a mother. The replacement of those grants with 'family credit' is a bitter joke both to families and to those who try to help them. Families rich enough to be credit-worthy are rich enough to buy a secondhand fireguard. Too poor for a low-interest loan from the DHSS, they now have no option but to go into debt on a credit card or pay usurious interest to the door-to-door peddlers of instant cash. Good citizens do not get into debt but good parents do not risk their toddler's safety.

New babies in the new decade

Most young people still take it for granted that they will eventually have children of their own yet few have any opportunity to form a realistic view of the difference a child will make to their lives. Preparation for Parenthood is a rare option in schools and where Childcare is taught it is usually a 'non-academic' option concentrating on techniques any parent learns in five minutes when the need arises, such as how to change a thoroughly soiled nappy without having to change all your own clothes. There are more important issues that should come first. Does s/he positively want to have children at all? If not, or not yet, is contraception an understood and available reality or crossed fingers and a giggle? If children are on his or her personal agenda, will a similar commitment be part of what s/he looks for in a partner? What kind of relationship does s/he foresee with a baby, toddler, child and adolescent, and has s/he considered how that relates to personal experience? And if s/he has not yet thought about the timing of a family, in relation to personal liberty, lifestyle or career, is s/he at least aware of their bearing on each other?

Planned or unplanned, pregnancy usually brings its own reward in interest and attention (whether congratulatory or condemnatory) from partners, families, friends and professionals. For many young women being pregnant is a first experience of female superiority and of acceptance as an equal — or at least a novitiate — by their own mothers and other adult women. As pregnancy progresses, antenatal care makes it clear that, courtesy of the potential baby she carries, she is, for the moment, important. Misleadingly, though, all this is preparation for the birth rather than for the child whose birthday it will be. Back home from the maternity hospital, often within two days of that physically and emotionally dramatic event, many women find all that concerned caring melting away to leave them literally holding the baby. Isolation and anticlimax are worse in the United States, where home-visits by nurses or breast-feeding counsellors are a privilege only of the rich and knowledgeable, than here, where community midwives, health visitors and voluntary organisations such as the National Childbirth Trust offer some postnatal support. There is not enough care for the new mother who must learn a new kind of caring. Some post-partum depression and anxiety is so common that we regard it as normal (or 'hormonal'). Yet the concept of 'baby blues' is almost inexplicable to women in more child-and-parent-friendly cultures. 'Are your women not glad to have a child?' they ask.

A new baby's needs are most likely to be met when the mother feels that he is part of herself, so that she scarcely distinguishes what he wants from what she wants, suffers when he suffers, and finds much of her pleasure and self-satisfaction in his contentment. This is the real meaning of that ill-used word 'bonding', a process that may indeed begin with a flash of recognition on the delivery table but which much more often evolves. If the baby remains external to the mother — an intruder into her self, her partnership and her life — he is, realistically, a very considerable nuisance. Once he is perceived as a nuisance, both parents may soon be appalled by his continual and unreasonable 'demands' and intent on modifying rather than meeting them. Professional support that assumes parents should put babies before themselves is then unusable. Many parents cannot put their babies first because they have no sense of ever having been first with anyone in their own infancy or of being first with anyone now. If anything can enable such a mother to pour out nurturance and care on her infant, it will be nurturance and care for herself. Very young mothers in particular, sometimes still facing the identity crises of adolescence, need mothering if they are to mother; loving if they are not to look to their babies for a kind of love infants do not have to give. And, despite our romantic expectations of couples being everything to each other, tragically few young men are capable of giving that kind of care to a partner or a baby since the macho tradition in which most are reared has demanded that they bury their own need to love and be loved and, with it, much of their capacity for tenderness. Many new fathers do not even have to face these demands on themselves as adult males because the workplace provides a socially acceptable, even compulsory, escape from emotional turmoil at home. How extraordinary that we now expect fathers to participate in the birth-drama and serve as their partner's anchor to reality during labour and delivery, but still do not expect, even allow them to take the same role during the life-drama of the following days. Our refusal to finance, or even discuss, paternity leave makes nonsense of our claims to support equally 'participant fatherhood' because it makes even those with the best intentions into part-time assistant mothers from the start.

Children whose emotional needs are not met are likely to become parents who find it hard to meet the emotional needs of their own children. Our society as a whole does not acknowledge those needs and therefore cannot recognise either the importance or the difficulty of the parenting role. It is that inimical context that makes it so difficult for professionals to advise, let alone intervene, on behalf of a child without being perceived as anti-parent. Two years ago a series of programmes for new parents on TV-AM brought thousands of letters at least half of which described the 'unreasonable demands' of babies and the 'unreasonable expectations' of health-care professionals:

> 'How can I teach my eight month son to play by himself? He's got toys and things but when I put him in his play-pen he keeps crying and if I put him on the floor he keeps trying to crawl after me. I've tried smacks and cuddles but he's getting worse. The Health Visitor says I should carry him about with me but he's spoilt enough already and anyway I've got other things to do.'

It is not that parents do not love their children; they almost always do. It is that a great many of them cannot like their children or enjoy living with them. Even parents who are less openly rejecting of infant needs are often inwardly resentful at children for ruining many aspects of their lives. They ruin partnerships (and are often a main cause of separation or divorce as well as a limiting factor in forming new relationships); they ruin friendships which, made at work, seldom survive the loss of proximity and mutual interests. They ruin careers — especially women's careers — and they ruin finances and lifestyles. And of course they add immeasurable stress to daily life lived in an environment that disregards them. With all that weighing against them, children have to bring tremendous emotional satisfaction to parents before the balance can be experienced as positive. Babies do not lie passively around waiting for parents to love them, of course. But a mother's day cannot be lit up by a first smile if she is not around to receive it and if she is not listening, those first conversational sounds and infectious giggles will be lost in background noise. Folklore declares that 'men like them better when they're a bit older.' Maybe it is not men (as opposed to women) who find it difficult to relate closely to young babies, but parents who are only with them after work and at weekends. If that is so, the current tendency to help mothers cope with the stresses of their unprepared, undervalued and underfunded role by getting out of it and back to the workplace may be contributing to a vicious circle. Maybe we should be looking instead for ways to re-value and refund the role itself.

3 Listening to children and representing them — a lawyer's view

Michael D. A. Freeman

Children are involved in a large variety of types of legal dispute. Questions arise as to whether they are in need of care or control, as to who should get custody of them or access to them, as to whether they should be adopted or have their surnames changed or be given a 'short, sharp shock' or be placed in secure accommodation or have their homes closed, or be allowed contraception without parental permission. The questions are almost limitless, but the answers in law, social policy and social work are far from unproblematic.

For too long the children themselves have taken a back seat in these disputes, sometimes so far back that even cries of anguish or protest have not been heard or noticed. Children are 'cases', 'problems', pieces of property, pawns to be moved about by others, but rarely persons or participants in a process affecting them.

Times are changing. There is a more active child advocacy movement than there has been in the past. There is the Children's Legal Centre. There is NAYPIC. It has become more meaningful to talk of children's rights.[1] Even the Butler-Sloss report can assert (albeit late in the report, for children are hardly its central focus) that children are persons, not objects of concern. For too long it notes 'the voices of the children were not heard'.[2] The *Gillick* case[3] is symptomatic of this change.

1989 saw the passing of a Children Act,[4] the first for 14 years. The 1975 Children Act was hailed as a children's charter.[5] Similar luxuriant phrases are being used this time. It is, of course, major legislation: little of either the private or public law of children remains untouched by it. To a large extent it does put children first. Thus, set out at the very beginning in Section 1 is the general principle that 'When a court determines any question with respect to — (a) the upbringing of a child...the child's welfare shall be the court's paramount consideration.'

In particular we are told the court shall have regard to 'the ascertainable wishes and feelings of the child concerned (considered in the light of his age and understanding)'.[6] There are six other matters listed but it is significant that the reference to 'wishes and feelings' is placed first. There are echoes of this provision throughout the Act (for example on the provision of accommodation,[7] in the duties of local authorities in relation to children looked after by them).[8] It may be said, and indeed it is true, that such provisions are little different from those in existing legislation. But they are found in a context where greater scope is given to the child to initiate, and to participate in, the decision-making process affecting him. For example, for the first time a child may apply to the court to ask for an order requiring a local authority in whose care he is to allow him contact with a parent,[9] a sibling or, indeed, anyone else. A child may also apply to have access stopped — a useful provision where a parent has re-married and the 'home' situation has changed drastically as a result.[10]

Children come in all shapes and sizes. The concept embraces a wide span of age. The problems in listening to a baby and a teenager are very different. But the same provisions apply to the toddler of seventeen months and the adolescent of seventeen years. It is for this reason that representation becomes so crucial an issue.

We have become used, since the implementation of the 1975 Act, to the separate representation of children,[11] to the acceptance of the notion that the interests of children and their parents are not necessarily coincident. Very little thought has been given to what representation of children involves — as to who should represent them and how. Rather more attention has been given to the issue in the United States in the wake of the notorious *Gault*[12] case in 1967, but even there the issues remain at best cloudy, and ambiguity often prevails.[13] We have become used also to the concept of the neutral social worker, the guardian *ad litem*, representing the child, often in conjunction with a solicitor. The solicitor is usually briefed by the social worker (one hardly needs to add that in many cases, necessarily so), though technically, of course, the solicitor's client is the child so that instructions should be issued by the child, wherever this is possible.

The inter-relationship is complex enough in practice, as anyone involved will have realised. What, for example, is the solicitor to do if her client does not agree with the social worker's assessment of what is best for him or herself? Take the example of the adolescent victim of sexual abuse: the social worker thinks care and removal from home is the best solution; the girl is 'prepared to take her chances' or she wants to stay put. The problem may be aggravated because her expressed preference may not be her real preference. As Anna Freud put it: 'Children of all ages have a natural tendency to deceive themselves about their motivations, to rationalise their actions, and to shy back from full awareness of their feelings, especially where conflicts of loyalty come into question'.[14] This is a stark confrontational example and it uses crude stereotypes. But it draws attention to a problem, and may give us some insight into what is involved in representation.

The debate and dilemma is relatively new in this arena but those familiar with political science or constitutional law will certainly recognise it.[15] Should MPs do what their constituents want or what they themselves think best? That is not a dispute which has been settled (the best never are). The dichotomy can be readily transposed to the question of children's representation. What is its function: is it to represent the child's best interests (his welfare) or to represent his wishes (his rights)? The dualism fits neatly into the debate about children's rights itself. Is this concerned with protecting children (with their 'salvation') or protecting their rights (with their 'liberation',[16] with autonomy)? The two sides of representation (as found in the debate about the role of MPs) find ready parallels in our context.

Take, for example, the question of *who* is to represent children: should representatives be drawn from the legal profession or from those whose primary expertise is in the field of social work? If the mandate view is adopted (that is to carry out constituents' wishes), the legal profession would seem to be the best qualified. If, on the other hand, the independence view is adjudged to prevail (that is the representative, having been elected or selected, does what he thinks best) social workers may have the edge (or at least so it is generally thought). One cannot come to a categorical answer for there are so many variables to consider: the age of the child or adolescent (is he or she in a position to give instructions?); the type of proceeding (note we have been assuming it is court-based but it could be administrative or legislative or use other fora); the procedural style adopted (is it accusatorial or inquisitorial?); the type of evidence being adduced; the orientation to be adopted by the representative (legalistic, social work, educational, etc.).

There is an informative study carried out in Connecticut which examined the role of attorneys who had represented children in divorce suits.[17] It is worth summarising because it throws much light on the problems of child representation. In essence, the investigators discovered that attorneys were confused about their role to the extent that they characterised it one way and acted inconsistently with this characterisation. They concluded that this confusion had been caused among other things by the 'shared assumption that custody adjudication fits one of the two standard models of litigation' and that

> ...either view of the child's representative — as adversarial advocate or inquisitorial factfinder — provides a misleading perspective on the position, for the child is not a party but rather is the individual whose interests must by law prevail. This undermines the adversarial assumptions of the advocate role, because a legal representative for the child's interests may as properly seek to instigate the adversary nature of the conflict as to participate in it. It also upsets the inquisitorial framework for the fact-finding role. Although the factfinder is introduced as an impartial investigator, he is to be impartial with regard to the parents, and even then, only initially. Entrusted with finding the information pertinent to the child's interests, the factfinder ends up looking very much like the advocate. The representative for a child serves as a preliminary decision-maker who evaluates the child's interests, since he is necessarily involved in sorting through competing psychological theories, ongoing tension between the rights of fathers and mothers, and shifting views on morality and lifestyles deemed harmful to children.[18]

The distinction drawn here is between fact-finder and advocate. Lawyers are better suited to the latter role, if for no other reason than that the stand they take is usually dependent on which protagonist enlists their aid. An investigator, by contrast, decides what he will advocate *a posteriori*, after examining all reasonably relevant facts. These American researchers found that their lawyers in their survey acted as 'pre-hearing factfinders, courtroom advocates, mediators, arbitrators, protectors and legal — and sometimes emotional — counsellors'.[19] They noted that if there was 'anything unique' about the role of lawyering for the child it was that 'the lawyer may be called on, in one litigation and with one client, to perform any or all these functions'.[20]

A number of roles have been identified. It may be useful to construct a schema of these. Three Canadian researchers (Dootjes, Erickson and Fox) have identified three models: the adversary, *amicus curiae*, and social work models.[21] The adversary role is traditionally combative — it envisages a lawyer using his skills within the framework of a trial governed by strict rules of law and procedure to convince a court that the cause for which he argues has merit and should prevail. The *amicus curiae* model is, to quote Bernard Dickens, 'comparably legalistic but neutral as to outcome'.[22] It envisages assistance to the court to resolve a conflict by presenting another perspective from the strictly partisan cases presented by the opposing parties. The social work model is intended to help the child 'by proposals, concession and collaboration to put into the most satisfactory condition that can be achieved'[23] (language reminiscent of Goldstein, Freud and Solinit's 'least detrimental alternative').[24]

Another way of conceiving models is to distinguish between those which regard the representative as an officer of the court and those which see him as independent of it. Yet another would contrast representatives in terms of their knowledge base and skills — those which believe the representative should have legal training and experience and those which envisage social work skills to be more valuable to the task. Some, of course, would prefer to construct a hybrid role, combining the skills of both professions.

It is clear that, if lawyers are to represent children, they require skills which the run-of-the-mill lawyer is apt to lack. Neither legal education nor training nor even the continuing specialist training given to those who opt to become child care specialists is adequate. Rarely does it penetrate into an understanding of child psychology. Too little insight into techniques of interviewing children are offered. Nor is this surprising given how inadequate a training is given to social workers and others whose daily task is to elicit from children what concerns them and what views they wish to express or get others to express on their behalf. The whole Cleveland episode is testimony to the ham-fisted way interviews, particularly the so-called 'disclosure' assessments, were conducted.[25]

It is important that someone representing a child should know, for example, how to interview him or her. This requires *inter alia*:

(i) The interviewer to be aware of his/her own biases.

(ii) The interviewer to minimise closed or leading questions, and avoid pressure, and ask open-ended questions. All of the research on memory and children as witnesses shows the most reliable information from young children comes from a condition of free recall.[26] Leading questions (and we know how common these are)[27] result in greater responses, but they greatly increase the chances of error.[28] What can we expect when a leading text (the CIBA one) advocates beginning a sexual abuse interview by saying something like, 'You told your teacher/granny/foster-mother that Daddy put his hand in your pants/showed you his penis, and that this was bothering you'.[29] Or, when a highly regarded US manual (by Sgroi) advises

3 Listening to children and representing them

interviewers to lie to a child to establish the credibility of the interviewer.[30] Such behaviours must inevitably reduce the validity and reliability of the assessment.

(iii) The interviewer to remain as objective and impartial as possible. This is, of course, difficult, given the harrowing circumstances in which the child may be. Oddly, it may be that this particular ability is one that lawyers are likely to find easier to cultivate than (for example) social workers.

(iv) The first session may have to be limited to establishing a relationship between the child and the interviewer, to get an impression of the child's level of development and capacities and to establish the child's expectations for what is going to happen subsequently. This is easier said than done. There is a premium on resources, undoubted shortages of guardians *ad litem* and specialist lawyers, and time is a precious resource. The establishment of a good relationship remains, however, essential if true communication is to result. It is impossible to listen to a child who is too anxious to settle or who is uncomfortable. The interviewer can also be overfriendly. What is required is warmth, support and empathy, but the interviewer must, nevertheless, remain in control.

(v) Interviewers should ask initially open-ended non-leading questions. If the allegation concerns sexual abuse, a 'Tell me about your father' is a better start than that commended in the CIBA publication or by Sgroi.

(vi) It requires also alertness to the cognitive and moral developmental level of the child. An example: up to about the age of six years, children confuse concepts that adults readily distinguish ('know', 'remember', 'guess', 'forget').[31] For this reason to ask a young child to remember what he said to others a couple of days ago (another parent, the police, a teacher, a social worker) may be counter-productive, though we all know it is common interviewing practice. The child may well be confused between a conversation and the reality of a prior event, for example, the abuse to which she has been subjected.

(vii) It is important also to minimise cues given to a child about what he or she is supposed to say. It is possible to supply information to the child in both obvious and subtle ways. I think a good example of this is the repetition of a question already answered by the child. We have all been made aware of Ronald Summit's 'sexual abuse accommodation syndrome'.[32] The syndrome has never been validated, yet it is widely adopted by professionals involved with sexual abuse allegations. Thus, the concept of secrecy (one of the five categories of behaviour that constitute the syndrome) is used to support the tactic of continuing to question when a child denies abuse. But, as Wakefield and Underwager rightly point out, applying the syndrome to children's statements 'means that nothing they say, nothing they do, can count against the belief that abuse happened'.[33] Acceptance of it can thus lead the questioner to ignore a child's denial and to persist in questioning until an affirmation is obtained. Non-verbal cues can also tell a child what the interviewer wants to hear. If we wish to listen to children, these are clearly things which must be avoided.

(viii) The interviewer must also remain calm and not show irritation when the child's response is not what is or was expected or desired. It is easy to get angry with a child, to express frustration, even to threaten or cajole. We know there are bad cases of this having happened in Cleveland, and it probably is not all that uncommon.

I have listed a number of the more obvious lessons for the interviewer to learn. I could list several others (e.g. the importance, often stressed by the courts, for videotape of the interview,[34] and the desirability of interviewing the child alone since the presence of another person may induce bias, distortions or omissions in the child's account and the error may be in either direction) and I could address the issue of some of the techniques employed like drawings, anatomically correct dolls etc. The latter I have discussed in detail elsewhere[35] and, though relevant to the representative's role, are more likely to be employed by paediatricians and others assessing whether abuse has taken place.

From what I have said, though, it should be clear that Genden's comment that 'a child may have less need for a litigation specialist than for a lawyer who has competence and familiarity with non-legal resources *must be right*.[36] Such a lawyer will also be able to distinguish between 'professionally informed belief' and 'personal value preferences'.[37] It is easy, as Winnicott wrote to 'decry or minimise the reality of a child's feelings'[38] or to disbelieve a child, as Cleveland and its aftermath amply demonstrate. It is a sad reflection of the times and the panic that, whereas once a child was disbelieved when she said she had been sexually abused, now it may be that there is a reluctance to disbelieve her when she denies she has been abused.[39] This is surely a poignant reminder to those who wish to establish a climate in which 'listening to children' becomes standard practice.

References

1. Freeman, M. D. A. (1983) *The Rights and Wrongs of Children*, Pinter.
2. *Report of the Inquiry into Child Abuse in Cleveland 1987* (1988), HMSO Cm. 412.
3. [1986] A. C. 112.
4. See Bainham, A. 'The Privatisation of the Family', (1990) *Modern Law Review*, vol. 53.

5. And see David Owen M.P.: 'A nation's children represent a nation's future. How society treats its own children is a good reflection of the overall health and stability of that society' (*Hansard*, H. C. vol. 893, vol. 1821).
6. See s. 1(3).
7. See s. 20(6) (a).
8. See s. 22(4) (a).
9. See s. 34(2).
10. See s. 34(4).
11. See s. 32A and B of Children and Young Persons Act 1969, introduced by s. 64 of the Children Act 1975.
12. 387 U.S. 1.
13. See Mnookin, R. *In The Interest of Children* (1985), W. H. Freeman. See also Goldstein, J. Freud, A. and Solnit, A. (1979) *Before The Best Interests of the Child*, Free Press, pp 111-129.
14. Freud, A. 'On the Difficulties of Communicating with Children' in Goldstein, J. and Katz, J. *The Family and the Law*, (1965) Free Press, p. 261.
15. See Arendt, H. (1982) *Representation*.
16. See Margolin, C. 'Salvation versus Liberation: The Movement for Children's Rights in a Historical Context', *Social Problems* vol. 22, p. 441 (1978).
17. Note 'Lawyering For The Child: Principles of Representation in Custody and Visitation Disputes Arising From Divorce.' *Yale Law Journal* vol. 87, p. 1126 (1978).
18. *Ibid*
19. *Ibid*
20. *Ibid*
21. 'Defence Counsel in Juvenile Court: A Variety of Roles', *Canadian Journal of Criminal Corrections*, vol. 14, p. 132 (1972). See also Stapleton, W. V. and Teitlebaum, L. (1972) *In Defense of Youth: A Study of the Role of Counsel in American Juvenile Courts*, Russell Sage Foundation, ch. 1.
22. See Dickens, B. 'Representing the Child in the Courts' in Baxter, M. and Eberts, M. (eds), *The Child and the Courts*, Carswell (1978) p. 273 at p. 280.
23. *Ibid*.
24. Goldstein *et al.*, *Beyond The Best Interests of The Child*, Free Press, (1973)
25. A series of cases looking at some of the problems is collected in [1987] 1 F.L.R. 269-346, especially *Re M* [1987] 1 F.L.R. 293. There is a good discussion of these by Douglas G. and Willmore C., 'Diagnostic Interviews as Evidence in Cases of Child Sexual Abuse', (1987) 17 *Fam. Law* 151. In *Re W*. [1]1990] 1 F.L.R. 203, Butler-Sloss L. J. viewed 'with some alarm' the use of the word 'disclosure' to identify an interview with a child for the purpose of eliciting whether or not there is something to disclose (p. 214).
26. Loftus, E. F. and Davies, G. M., 'Distortions in the Memory of Children', *Journal of Social Issues* vol. 40(2), pp 51-67 *(1984)*.
27. See *Re H* [1987] 1 F.L.R. 332; *Re W*. [1987] 1 F.L.R. 297; *C* v *C* [1987] 1 F.L.R. 321; *Re N* [1987] 1 F.L.R. 280; [1987] 1 F.L.R. 293.
28. Dent H. R. and Stephenson G. M., 'An Experimental Study of the Effectiveness of Different Techniques of Questioning Child Witnesses' *British Journal of Social and Clinical Psychology* vol. 18 pp 41-51 (1979).
29. See (ed) Porter R., (1984) *Child Sexual Abuse Within the Family*, Tavistock, p. 69.
30. See Sgroi S. M., (1982) *Handbook of Clinical Intervention in Child Sexual Abuse*, Lexington Books.
31. Wellman H. M. and Johnson C. N., 'Understanding of Mental Processes: A Developmental Study of "Remember" and "Forget"', *Child Development*, vol. 50, pp 79-88 (1979).

32. Summit, R.C. (1983) 'The Child Sexual Abuse Accommodation Syndrome', *Child Abuse and Neglect* vol. 7, pp 177-193.
33. Wakefield, H. et al (1988) *Accusations of Child Sexual Abuse*, C. C. Thomas, p. 215.
34. *Re N* [1987] 1 F.L.R. 293; *Re Z* [1989] 2 F.L.R. 3. But in *Re W* [1990] 1 F.L.R. 203 it was said that 'its status cannot be greater than other statements of children, although its impact...is more direct'. (*per* Butler-Sloss L. J. at p. 214).
35. Freeman, M. D. A., 'Cleveland, Butler-Sloss and Beyond — How Are We To React to the Sexual Abuse of Children?' *Current Legal Problems* p. 85 at pp 111-114 (1989).
36. Genden, J. K. 'Separate Legal Representation for Children: Protecting The Rights and Interests of Minors and Judicial Proceedings', *Harvard Civil Rights — Civil Liberties Law Review*, vol. 11, p. 565 at p. 589 (1976).
37. *Per* Goldstein J., Freud A., Solnit, A. J. and Goldstein S. (1986) *In The Best Interests of The Child*, Free Press, p. 120.
38. Winnicott, C. (1964) *Social Work in Child Care*, Bookstall Publications, p. 43.
39. See, in support, the observation of Bush J. in *Re Z* [1989] 2 F.L.R. 3, 10.

Part 2
Agencies which serve children

4 Telling tales: in and out of school

Michael Marland and Gill Malcolm

The school as a listening community

Sadly, schools are not well placed to listen to children, except in response to a teacher's subject-orientated questions, because of our training, attitudes, facilities, schedules, and staffing patterns. Much is achieved by sensitive teachers, but one has to admit that this is despite, not because of, the system. None of us in teaching would wish to admit anything other than caring for the child, but the reality of the extent of our real listening is far from that ambition.

There is no doubt that, like other occupations, teaching can become what I have come to call 'professio-centric'. The Head who declared in the witness box of the Auld Enquiry, 'Parents? Don't talk to me about parents, we're the pros in this business' (Auld 1976)[1] would have wished to have been thought 'child-centred' but, as so often, was actually trapped in a professio-centrism of his own making. I once worked with a teacher who resigned her responsibility position because in a particular dispute 'the child was put before the teacher.'

Of course, all of us under stress will look inward and become self- and group-protective, and the endemic under-resourcing of schools creates unnecessary stress. Lack of support staff, lack of time, inadequate electronic communication facilities, often poor physical accommodation and sketchy institutional planning all harass the teacher and thus make her or him less amenable to hearing pupil messages.

A different problem is the inadequate incorporation of the

Education Welfare Service and its members in the work of too many schools. We could learn so much from the different but complementary professional stance of Education Welfare Officers. They are essentially client-centred, with the pupil as their client, and their training and experience could help teachers listen to children if we listened to them.

So could a fuller, more sensitive, and more generous listening to parents and guardians. It is often forgotten in the rather closed world of schools that parents are our legal clients — the law requires *parents* to educate their children, though most use schools as their *agents*. Our approach to children is subtly but deeply affected by the too easy assumption that young people are in school compulsorily and by our choice — not that of their parents. The fact that parents have chosen a school, *our* school, should lead us to a greater openness.

Only too often one whole aspect of schooling is totally forgotten — the power of those who are not teachers. Our crude teacher/non-teacher dichotomy is unhelpful and rapidly becoming downright pointless. Office staff, schoolkeepers, secretaries, and others all contribute to the listening power of the school as a whole.

Of course, there is much sensitivity and intelligence in teachers, and often a professed willingness to listen — but while this is necessary it is not sufficient. A school must not take for granted either the willingness of the teacher to listen or the pupil to talk, nor assume the possibility. Instead, a school should carefully define its aims and out of those consciously plan to *empower* the pupil to talk. This requires a clear programme to enable the pupil to grow in understanding of her or himself: you cannot talk about your needs if you cannot explore and define them.

Thus the issue of 'listening to children' inevitably encompasses its opposite, but complementary side, that is, enabling pupils in school to *talk*. That is both a pastoral care and curriculum matter.

Contrary to much professional fear, an apparently unrelated number of central influences are currently encouraging pastoral care (cf. Marland, 1989b);[2] including the specific inclusion in the *Schoolteachers' Pay and Conditions Document* (DES 1987)[3] of 'pastoral care', clear HMI leadership, Home Office Section II Guidelines: and the Department of Education and Science/National Curriculum Council's promulgation of Personal and Social Education. Indeed Section 1 of the Education Reform Act 1988 is definitely 'pastorally' orientated.

One can begin to chart the requirements of a school in which teachers can most successfully listen to children as follows:—

1. A coherent pastoral-care scheme, in which home liaison,

guidance, welfare, discipline, and individual support are inter-related.
2. A pastoral programme in which individual case-work pastoral care is complemented by a coherent pastoral curriculum (cf. Marland, 1981[4] and 1989b[2]), which includes relevant concepts, language, self-awareness, and self-esteem. This would encourage talking *with* and not merely *at*, enabling true talk by the child.
3. The creation of *occasions* for talk. Serendipity is inadequate for this, and snatched conversations in classroom and corridor a poor context of real listening.

Although all teachers have an important listening role, in the secondary school this focuses on the Tutor as the key listener. 'The Tutor is a teacher whose subject is the pupil herself,' as I have put it elsewhere (Marland, 1989, p.iii).[5] The same is true of the 'class teacher' in the junior school. The continuous class meetings make the class-teacher's task easier in a number of respects. On the other hand, the very wide-ranging responsibilities and the hugely heterogeneous curriculum content for which she or he is responsible in some ways diffuses the essential 'personal education' curriculum focus; in contrast, the Tutor is there for no other purpose and has timetabled and labelled time.

There are, though, four capital problems in developing the Tutor as the key listener:

(a) The lack of preparation and training for teachers in the pastoral aspect of the school.
(b) The frequent curriculum vacuum in education about self and the fracture between pastoral care and curriculum.
(c) The lack of time.
(d) The poor facilities.

The structure and curriculum of pastoral care

A planned pastoral curriculum links the individual to the group in a programme and shifts pastoral care from reactive to proactive, thus making the purpose and the opportunities for listening more numerous, better prepared for, more realistic, and richer.

The tutorial/pastoral aim is to enable the individual to be more fully and truly her- or himself and to develop an understanding of and respect for others. Just as frustration for the Tutor and starvation for the tutee comes from a well intentioned but essentially ill-designed and impractical attempt to offer tutorial pastoral care only through one-to-one discussion, so whole-group tutoring cannot complete the task alone.

Much of the Tutor's work requires individual, one-to-one 'counselling': very often pupils will need talking with and will benefit from a conversation with their Tutor. Such conversations, in snatched moments, after school, or in a methodically planned series of 'review' meetings, sometimes involve questioning, sometimes advising, sometimes exhorting, and often passing on ideas or facts which the pupil needs for his own decision-making. They are an essential extension of and complement to the whole-group tutoring. Indeed there is a sense in which the latter under-pins or serves the former. It is clearly a weakness of the UK school systems that such crucial individual sessions are not budgeted for, and neither structured nor scheduled. Over the year there should be reciprocal relationship between individual and whole-group tutorial programme work, with the former sometimes prompting and illuminating the latter, and in its turn the programme being called upon in individual counselling.

If the tutee is to recognise and change his behaviour, he needs to be able to stand outside, as it were, and look on as a spectator. One help towards this is the provision of data on the behaviour of others. If the tutee is to be able to achieve this, she or he must be able to make for her — or himself best use of the school, to 'exploit' it, if you like. To be a successful student, the child has to learn how to be a pupil — a huge and complex learning task. This is the Tutor's role of 'educational guidance'.

The key aspects of these explorations are obvious: the Tutor should take the initiative. This requires advising strategies to enable the group and individuals to find ways to deepen their understanding of self and others, and eventually to become both willing and able to take control of self.

Much tutoring is signalling the fact that the ordinary choices made in school are a paradigm of life. The mutually respecting group led by the sensitive but intellectually clear Tutor will move from the group's present to experiences as presented for objective study from the small to the large, and from the particular to the general. Overall, the Tutor will enable the members of the group to develop their own ideas and strategies. Exhortations will fall away as the tutee is enabled to find strategies. This enabling cannot be left to the serendipity of daily happenings, but has to be planned. This is the 'curriculum' aspect of pastoral care in general and within that, of tutoring, and it is out of such planning that the 'tutorial programme' is devised.

The curriculum will include learning and study itself; sexuality, which will be considered early enough and fully enough to be looked at when or even before it is required; adult relationships; and behaviour generally. parenthood and the home, school, society, neighbourhoods — all these aspects of the child's life should be part of the curriculum. Thus analysis of the school, views on its methods, teachers, procedures, and atmosphere would be made conscious for consideration and thus discussion. This curriculum approach shifts the Tutor's role 'from exhortation to enabling'.

A further aspect is the school's relationship to parents and homes; the school that does not listen to parents is unlikely to be one of effective listeners to children. We are not very good at home–school relationships, despite our hopeful rhetoric, as Alastair Macbeth (1989)[6] has demonstrated in *Involving Parents*.

Creating time and space to listen

After attitude, curriculum, and skills, the most important aspect is the simple one of *time*. Listening implies talking, and talking requires time. The class teacher is the key professional in the junior school, and yet what is her or his workload, and how much time is available for one-to-one communication? Similarly, the Tutor in the secondary school is the key person, and she or he requires planned, bespoke time. Pastoral care on the corridor run is the sadly bizarre norm for a 'communication situation'! The school week is usually too frenetic for listening and the follow-ups to listening.

One way of considering school organisation from the point of view of listening to children is to ponder the sheer number of interchanges in a day; teacher–child and teacher–adult interchanges are so numerous that it is difficult for most to be either sustained or deep. One report of a general inspection of a secondary school included the comment that could be true of so many schools. 'Many problems are literally dealt with in passing' (ILEA, 1986, p.11).[7]

The route towards a solution requires the planning of meetings, which need to be full-group, small-group, and individual. These should not be merely re-active but also planned as 'review sessions', that is regular private meetings in pleasant surroundings which are conducive to relaxed talking and listening. The need is to create a relatively safe environment. Such occasions allow the child to talk as a pupil unstressed by a specific event or an impending decision.

Less easy to arrange is the ambience of a residential centre. Living together, studying, and making a variety of visits, pupils and teachers establish an extended and somewhat different relationship, one which can lead to both fuller talking and more sensitive listening. I have come to call a suitable residential centre 'a laboratory for pastoral care'. Most of these meetings will be with the pupils alone, but occasionally they should be with parents present.

The child–parent group sometimes leads the pupils to revelations, ideas, or comments that might not arise otherwise.

For this purpose, home visits have some special advantages for listening to children. Of course, the presence of parents can create an inhibition. Nevertheless, because the teacher is the 'guest' and the family in control of seating, refreshments, and atmosphere children will often be not so much more forthcoming as *differently* forthcoming. I judge that I have fairly often heard things said by pupils when I have been talking in their homes that I should not hear in school — and that we have all benefited.

An extreme example of the value of listening to parents and pupils together is given by the child psychiatrist, Whilom Yule, when he was endeavouring to help the girls who survived the sinking of the *Jupiter*. He stressed that by seeing and listening with parents and pupils initially in separate groups and then together they were able 'to share publicly some of their feelings', and he significantly added: 'Hopefully, that gave permission for such discussions to take place more readily at home' (Yule, 1989, p.5).[8]

Conclusion

One way of categorising a school is to think of it as 'a listening community'. To help a school develop as such requires:—

1. Development in teacher education, including in-service professional development.
2. A curriculum developed to include 'personal and social education', the 'pastoral' aspect of the curriculum.
3. A coherent pastoral care policy and procedures.
4. A close involvement with parents.
5. The costing in and planning of meetings.

All this *can* be done, and a school should plan to develop its listening capacity, assess its 'listening quotient', and be proud of this aspect of its work.

The School Nurse's role

The School Nurse has a very particular role in listening to children, as she spends the major part of her professional life in direct contact with them. Unlike the health visitor she tends to see children without parents present, and therefore forms a direct bond with the child. Children will often see their school nurse as somebody they can confide in, who is separate from the school structure and not in a position of authority, but who is sympathetic and understanding. The school nurse is in a key position in the area of Child Protection because she can build up relationsips with children based on trust. She is a professional, whilst retaining the image prevalent in society of being the 'angelic carer' who will be there, understand and 'make it better'.

There are many factors which determine the effectiveness of the School Nurse in listening to children, however — both practical and personal — and also changes which could usefully be made to enhance the process by which children communicate with the nurse and thereby facilitate the prevention of child abuse and the protection of the child.

Practical issues

For the child in school, accessibility to the School Nurse is essential. This is necessarily limited by school hours and timetables and to some extent by the structure, management and ethos of the school. The nurse is a guest within the school and must work within the limits they impose. From experience, one of the major hurdles to overcome can be the initial reaction of the Headmaster and his/her expectations of the nurse's role. If they believe you are there to check for headlice and arrange medical and immunisation sessions only, then they are often shocked by your request for 'surgery times' and groupwork sessions to be timetabled in. It is important to get a key member of staff to support you, who understands what you are trying to achieve and why.

In one school a weekly group of eight girls who had all been abused in various ways was established by the School Nurse. The importance of attending all sessions and of good timekeeping was impressed on the group and the only occasions on which they could not attend, or arrive late were when they had been directed by teachers to 'clear the playground' or to run a message for somebody. The school simply did not understand that the group was in any way different from a normal school lesson.

The other extreme is when a school is desperate for somebody to take on a pastoral role and tries to use the nurse inappropriately as a kind of school social worker.

The nurse must be clear about what role she is taking, what she wants to achieve and why and how she will do it. The formation of a clear plan for each school from the beginning will enable the nurse to plan her time so that she is available as much as possible for the child to contact when he/she wishes.

Surgery times give a clear opportunity for children to approach the nurse in confidence and privacy. If they know that the nurse will be in the same place at the same time every day with time for them, then they are able to feel safe and secure in the knowledge that when the time is right for them to speak they will be given the opportunity. As a School Nurse I used to work in a special school for children who had medical and social/emotional problems, and I attended every day at the same time and sat in the same room, in which it was possible to be private and not too uncomfortable.

One particular girl (I will call her Sonia) used to visit me every day for about eighteen months. Some days she only wanted a cuddle, some days she just cried and on occasions she told me some minor details about her home life. Her mother left when she was very young and she lived with her father, brother and a male lodger. She was now fourteen and desperate for some female advice and guidance. She was enuretic on occasions and she had just started menstruating, neither of which she could talk to her father about. If her bed got wet or bloodstained then she would just leave it and get back into it the next night. The school believed her problems to be due to lack of mothering, which to a large extent they were, but over a period of time a story was building up. She discussed at great length her unspecified fears of going to bed, her inability to get to sleep which she later said was due to scratching at her door, and her great fear of men. I referred her on through the social worker to the Child Guidance unit where she is now seen by an experienced counsellor and, I hope, able to disclose what she has been trying to say for so long. For girls like Sonia there must be someone who is able and willing to listen when the time is right for the child.

It is not always the case that schools provide a space which is conducive to communicating with children. In one school the only access to space was to move the school secretary out of her office at a pre-arranged time and date, along with her typewriter and filing cabinet! In another school the ceiling of the medical room was in danger of collapsing and so the room could not be used for a year. Some medical rooms in schools are very cold and cheerless and associated in a child's mind with examinations and injections. If possible the introduction of some floor cushions, posters on the wall and some carpets can transfer the atmosphere, and make the room more inviting to children, parents and staff.

Listening skills

Moving away from practical considerations, we come to the more complex and problematic issues which may affect the School Nurse's ability to communicate effectively with children. The nurse herself may not really want to hear what a child may need to tell her. It is very easy to divert potentially difficult conversations before they really start and to get on to more tangible topics which are within the nurse's experience and control. It is much more comfortable for nurses to feel that they are in control of a situation and therefore to take the lead in a conversation and be directive.

So it does not always come easily to really listen, to allow the child to be in control, to be non-directive, to move at the child's pace and to allow the child to express very difficult and uncomfortable emotions which the nurse does not have the power to heal immediately. There have been occasions when I have felt that a child has wanted to disclose something to me and I have had my overbooked diary running through my head, and secretly thinking, 'Not now...please, not now.'

The time that a child needs to talk will not fit in to your schedule, it will never be convenient, but it is the right time for that particular child and it is so important that the nurse appears to be completely receptive and to have all the time in the world for that child, even if this is not actually the case. Body language can be important here. There is no point in saying, 'Of course I'm not in a rush,' whilst you are frantically collecting your papers together, jotting down a few notes in some records and checking your diary. To properly listen one must relax and give one's undivided attention to what one is being told.

The most daunting part of listening is the worry that you may say the wrong thing and stop the flow, or give the wrong prompt which inhibits rather than enables. Sometimes the fear that you may not react in the right way may inhibit your natural reaction which may well be most useful.

Obviously all children are individual and so each response is individual. Two very different examples of this are as follows: first, a teenage girl who decided to disclose to me that her father and mother both used to beat her severely. She began talking in a very boastful and insolent way about how tough she was and how she terrorised the girls in her class. I felt that she really wanted me to like her and was testing me out to see whether I did. She was telling me all the worst things about herself to see when I started to look disgusted or horrified. I was helped by the fact that I really did like her and I'm sure she knew this and so felt that she could trust me.

The second example was a very timid and scared seven-year-old whom I felt needed some encouragement, as well as a lot of empathic silence. It was with this particular case that I felt very concerned that I might interrupt his flow of thought and speech, and even during the long silences I felt it was right to keep silent.

In other situations I have felt that gentle talk to ease the situation for the child was useful for them giving them reassurance and confidence. I would tell them that I am on their side, whatever has happened; that I won't be shocked by whatever it is they wish to tell me; that other children have experienced the same things, and that it is very brave to be able to speak out so that someone can help them stop what is happening to them; that whatever it is that is happening is definitely not their fault and they are in no way to blame.

I also explain that I have to pass on what they will tell me to someone who is in a better position to help them but that if they want me to, I will stay with them during this and will always be on their side. I would advise School Nurses to be clear that this was in fact possible before they promise it, since not all Social Workers will allow this to happen, or it may just not be practically possible. In this situation I feel that it should be made a priority that whoever the child chooses to disclose to and feels most comfortable with should, if at all possible, be with the child throughout the subsequent investigation. This obviously has implications for the management of professionals who are likely to be put in this situation, but I feel it is in the child's best interests and therefore should be part of the procedure to be followed.

Changes

There are changes which can be made to the present setting within schools which can facilitate the process of allowing children to speak and giving them the right to be listened to. It is vital that all School Nurses are adequately trained in Child Protection issues. They must be given the opportunity to develop listening skills and a sound knowledge base of procedures and their implications for children. Unless they are clear that the child's interests are always paramount, they can all too easily lose sight of the real issues in the general rush of events and emotions surrounding disclosures of child abuse.

They must be clear about their role generally and in relation to child protection, so that they can make adequate assessments of situations and pass on information at the right time, to the right person, in a clear and concise way. They must, on the one hand, be confident enough to take on direct face-to-face work with children whilst, on the other hand, being clear about the limitations of their role.

There are many factors, particularly in a deprived, inner city area, which will affect a child's ability and inclination to talk and the nurse's ability and inclination to listen effectively. There may be a high proportion of ethnic children who do not have English as their first language. Social factors, culture and religion can influence the views of both children and workers as to what is abusive. Again, training and Health education, looking at attitudes and beliefs, where they come from and how they fit in to the values of society as a whole, are needed within schools and as a prerequisite of training courses for School Nurses.

For instance, what is our attitude as child protection workers to children who may be treated according to their countries' customs, perhaps whilst away from this country, in a manner which is not accepted in our culture (for example, female circumcision)? Or again, where ethnic children are physically abused, perhaps by being beaten with a stick, do we act to protect the rights of such a child or do we accept the view of the adults concerned that such behaviour is acceptable discipline within their culture? Such dilemmas need to be faced and resolved by all of us involved in working for the welfare of children.

The position of children in our society is an issue which will only be changed by a consistent effort on the part of all professionals to raise awareness of how our attitudes as a society directly affect the wellbeing of our children. We need to be prepared and able to listen to what they have to tell us and to act sympathetically and speedily to ensure that their best interests are always paramount.

References

1. Auld, Robin (1976) *Auld Report, Report on the public inquiry conducted by Robin Auld QC, into the Teaching Organisation and Management of the William Tyndale Junior and Infant Schools, Islington, London N1, ILEA.*
2. Marland, Michael (1989b) *The Shaping and Delivery of Pastoral Care in Education*, Vol. 8, No. 1, (Winter 1989).
3. *School Teachers' Pay and Condition Document* (1987), DES.
4. Marland, Michael (1981) 'The Pastoral Curriculum,' in Best, et. al., *Perspectives on Pastoral Care*, Heinnemann Organisation in School Services.
5. Marland, Michael, (1989a), *The Tutor and the Tutor Group*, Longman Tutorial Resources.
6. Macbeth, Alastair (1989) *Involving Parents*, Heinemann Educational Books.
7. Report on School (1986) ILEA.
8. Yule, William, 1989, 'The Effects of Disaster on Children,' in *Newsletter*, Association for Child Psychology and Psychiatry, Vol. 11, No. 8, (November 1989).

5 Active listening — a social services' perspective

Jan Thurgood

Introduction

The basic premise of this chapter is that listening to children is essential and central to all aspects of Social Services child care work, which includes child protection and work with children who are looked after by local authorities.

A Child in Trust, the report of the enquiry into the death of Jasmine Beckford, provides a stark reminder of the consequences of social work practice that focuses insufficiently on the child[1]. The report criticises social workers and other professionals for failing to chart indicators of concern, such as medical evidence of failure to thrive in height and weight, and for not ensuring that the child in need of protection had relationships with workers, which could provide both monitoring of the child's welfare and an avenue for the disclosure of abuse.

To ensure that children are protected and receive good enough care, social workers have to obtain a comprehensive picture of the child's development, functioning and needs, and also provide a structure of work wherein the child has consistent relationships with professional staff, who seek actively to hear the child's perspective.

The legislation and regulations, within which social workers operate, impose a requirement to take into account the views of children in making decisions on their upbringing. The Children Act 1989 states that the 'ascertainable wishes and feelings of the child (considered in the light of his age and understanding)' must be taken into account when decisions on Orders and adoptions are made by Courts and when other major decisions are made about a child's upbringing.[2]

This chapter explores a range of techniques for facilitating communication with children. Many different workers within Social Service Departments listen to children in a variety of settings. Children may be seen individually, in groups and, in the process of work, with a whole family. Work with a child should go hand-in-hand with work undertaken with the child's family of origin and/or current carers. It is not possible to understand a child's communication unless it is set in the context of his or her daily living situation, past experiences and racial and cultural background.

The process of listening to a child is a dynamic one. The fact that a worker listens has an impact on the child and family. A worker is not a passive recipient of information, but is often in the role of giving information. For instance, the worker has to explain his or her own powers and duties. Setting up a relationship with a child and family in order to listen, also offers the potential for therapeutic intervention. From the outset, a worker needs to be thinking about how to produce positive change.

Both social work practice and the policy making of Social Services Departments should be informed by listening to children. It is a truism worth stating that the experience of working directly with children provides an essential element in the development of a practitioner's understanding and skills.

Listening to children can alter the practice of social workers, Social Services Departments and of other agencies. For example, it was listening to the experience of children who gave evidence in the prosecution of sexual offenders that prompted changes in court room procedure to allow children to give evidence on video links. Individuals and groups of children living in local authority provision can make telling comments on the quality of care based on their own experiences. Local authorities need to actively elicit these comments and adapt policy and practice in their light.

Statutory duties in local authority social work and listening to children

Each Social Services Department employs a wide range of people with varied roles and responsibilities, who provide different types of services to children and families. These include foster carers, childminders, nursery and residential staff, Intermediate Treatment workers, family and day centre staff, family aides and field social workers, based in hospitals and area offices. The task of each offers

5 Active listening

important opportunities for listening to children.

The statutory aspect of local authority work has prominence in the media and probably in the mind of the general public. It raises particular issues in terms of listening to children. While a wide range of workers can be involved in cases, where the local authority has statutory powers and responsibilities it is the field social worker who will generally hold case accountability and will, therefore, be most closely identified with the exercise of statutory powers.

Any professional who has the task of listening to children has at the outset to explain to the child and the child's carer the nature of his or her professional role and responsibilities. Parents and children need to understand the nature and extent of the powers of a worker, who is carrying out statutory duties. The reality and the client's perception of these powers will influence the process of listening to children. The social worker must also be clear that her priorities must be with the child in any possible conflict between the interests of the parents and of the child. The legal and procedural framework within which social workers operate is inevitably complex. Clients require clear verbal and written explanations of Court Proceedings; procedures relating to children who are looked after by the local authority and information about Child Protection Registration. Information has to be accessible to the family and the child. This means, where necessary, translation into the first language of the family and also putting it into words that young children can grasp.

There are certainly circumstances, where concerns over a worker's statutory powers lead families and children to be guarded in their communication with social workers. It is important that their perception of such powers is realistic and not exaggerated. Equally, children with a clear perception of a worker's role being to protect them from harm and abuse can and do use relationships with social workers to disclose abuse.

There are two key aspects to be considered in listening to children in statutory work. The first is to ensure that all information relevant to a child's safety, welfare and development is co-ordinated. The second is to consider who is to work directly with the child to listen to the child's wishes, feelings and experiences.

Information relevant to a child's safety, welfare and development will include a detailed history of the child's physical, emotional, educational and social development. Particular reference has to be made to any incidents of physical, sexual and/or emotional abuse and to separations from key attachment figures, losses and moves. It will also involve an assessment of the child's current physical, emotional and educational functioning and needs and a detailed picture of the child's behaviour in a variety of settings. Emphasis must be placed on an assessment of the child's sense of self-worth and identity which includes cultural, racial and religious identity. The worker needs also to gain a clear picture of the child's key relationships and the quality of these.

Comprehensive information on a child's development and needs has to go hand-in-hand with a full assessment of the child's home situation and of a carer's capacity to meet those needs. This includes not only an assessment of the carers' current functioning, but also an awareness of the carers' own experiences of parenting in their childhood, and of their parenting of other children. Social workers have to test out the capacity of carers to change in their parenting if there are problems, and to recognise what practical and therapeutic services will enable a parent to cater better for their child's needs.

When a number of children in a family are in need of protection or are being looked after by a local authority, the needs of each child have to be considered in detail. For example, one child in a family may have a specific difficulty in relationship with a parent not shared by other children. In making decisions on children's upbringing, however, there must be recognition of the importance of maintaining ties and bonds between siblings.

In collating information on a child, a social worker will be drawing on information from a range of workers from within and beyond the Social Services Department and, most importantly, on information gathered from the family and child.

The role of the statutory worker in working directly with children can vary. As a principle of practice, I would stress that a worker who holds case accountability should aim to build a relationship of significance with each child for whom he or she is responsible and who is of an age where relationship is possible. There are times when this is impracticable. In times of staff shortage, workers do not have time. In other circumstances, the conflicts of loyalties generated for children in statutory cases mean that either the child needs a worker different from the person who works with his or her parents or the child may reject the person whom he or she sees as most responsible for the statutory intervention in their life.

It is often useful, therefore, that a child is designated his or her own worker. This may sometimes be another field social worker and in cases where parents have many needs or, for instance, mental health problems, the model of allocation of a field social worker for the child and another for the parent is successful as long as the workers are in regular contact.

It is more often the case, however, that a child builds the strongest attachments to those with whom he/she spends most time. A child looked after by the local authority will generally have the strongest attachments to those with whom he/she lives. A child in need of protection, who attends day nursery or school, will likewise often communicate most freely with teaching or nursery staff.

One of the essential skills of the statutory worker is to be able to draw out the listening to children done by others. The beginning of this process lies in demonstrating the value placed on the observations and assessments of others and in opening avenues to good inter-disciplinary working. This process has to be undertaken at all levels in Social Services Departments: from the setting up of clear inter-agency guidelines for investigating child abuse to social workers on individual cases spending time getting to know the teachers, day nursery staff, child minders foster carers and residential staff who have key relationships with the child.

Social workers have to draw out and clarify the concerns of others. If, for example, a teacher reports that a child has 'disclosed sexual abuse', a social worker will need to elicit from the teacher a detailed account of the child's disclosure which as nearly as possible relies on the child's words. The worker will want to hear the teacher's observations of the child's emotional state at disclosure and in general. It would be important to hear any concerns the teacher has about the child's development and behaviour and to help the teacher reflect on whether there have been any recent changes of significance in the child's behaviour or home circumstances. The worker should also elicit the teacher's knowledge of the child's family and cultural background and explore the teacher's views of the strength of family relationships for the child. The social worker's task is to help the referrer be specific about concerns, but also to gain a broad span of information about the child and his/her social context.

Listening to children and working with families

A full understanding of a child's communication can only be achieved when it is set within the context of his/her real world experiences and relationships. Listening to children has to take place in a structure of work which acknowledges this.

Child care legislation and policy making are increasingly reinforcing the principle that Social Service provision should seek to promote parents' sense of responsibility and competence. In most cases the aims of listening to children and enhancing parental competence will be congruent, but we have to be aware of the circumstances when this is not the case and to strike an appropriate balance. Natural parents can feel undermined by their children forming strong relationships with professional workers. Social workers have to have as good skills in working with parents in such situations as they do with children.

It is possible for workers to ally with a child in a way that will not be helpful to the family as a whole or in the long-term interests of the child. For example, in work with teenagers where there are issues of a young person challenging parental authority, workers need to listen to the child and be sure to pick up specific issues of concern for the child's protection and welfare, but they need also to support and strengthen appropriate parental authority.

There are clearly advantages in listening to children in the course of work undertaken with a whole family. Patterns of interaction between family members can be observed and changed. Parents can be given help to build on parenting skills and explore difficulties in relationships. In cases where the concerns that led to intervention were abuse of a child or concern over development, it is essential to maintain the focus on the child by having a contract with the family where the measure of successful outcome is seen in terms of the cessation of abuse or the improved development of the child.

The above may seem self-evident but often in work with families where severe abuse occurs, parents deny the abuse and are unwilling to engage in work that addresses it. Clearly such denial has to lead to serious consideration about whether a child can be adequately protected within their family.

In most cases, social workers can work in open partnership with parents on joint issues of concern. There are, however, situations where severe abuse of children occurs, when social workers have to be aware not only of the denial of abuse by parents, but also that children are placed under powerful injunctions to maintain silence.

A child may be told that the consequences of disclosure of abuse are repeated or further abuse or removal of self or another family member from the home. Some children feel guilty and personally responsible for the abuse and so do not disclose. Other children meet with disbelief when they make initial attempts to disclose. In these circumstances, workers and agencies have to think how in a range of ways to demonstrate to children and adults that abuse can be acknowledged and addressed.

At a general level, organisations such as 'Childline' play an important part in making children aware that it is possible to acknowledge abuse. Programmes in schools that teach children how to keep safe also serve this purpose. On an individual case level, we have to ensure children have access to adults who are ready to listen. We need to be alert to indicators of abuse in a child's behaviour and physical and emotional presentation. It is important to consider at what point these indicators provide a sufficiently high degree of concern to raise with the child and parent the question of possible abuse.

5 Active listening

In my own practice, I was influenced by the comments of a six-year-old, who had been the subject of severe and persistent sexual abuse. Although colleagues and I had worked with her on an intensive basis and had major concerns about her emotional development and behaviour, including an age-inappropriate sexual knowledge, it had taken an external event to reveal the abuse. After the disclosure, she talked of her feelings that she should have disclosed the abuse at an earlier stage. I felt that the responsibility lay with ourselves as adults to have raised the question of abuse with her and at least to have opened the possibility of her making a disclosure.

Repeated attempts to obtain disclosure from a child can in themselves be abusive. There are some cases where workers have many indications that abuse, particularly sexual abuse, has been or is occurring, but no means of verifying this. In these circumstances, often the only way forward is to provide a consistent relationship to the child where abuse could be disclosed if the child so chose. It is only by listening keenly to children that a balance between intrusion and the compounding of denial can be achieved.

Ways of listening

Staff in Social Services Departments employ a wide range of skills and techniques in listening to children. We listen to children with our ears, eyes and even sometimes via the bruises on our shins. It requires emotional sensitivity, and clear thinking and reflection, to understand the meaning of communications and behaviours.

There is much scope and need for imaginative and creative approaches which are adapted to the child and fit with the worker's task and style of working. Many of the children who come to the attention of Social Services Departments have been subject to abuse and neglect. They may have had no consistency in relationships with adults or have been rejected. Their experiences may give them little reason to trust adults and many, particularly teenagers, have a strong sense of alienation from the adult world.

The success of any attempt to listen to children depends on the worker becoming a sufficiently reliable and consistent figure in the child's world. Constant changes of worker or a pattern of irregular, late or broken appointments will produce feelings in the child that no-one has real concern for them. To develop relationships with children for whom rejection and adult abuse have been commonplace, we have to demonstrate our reliability and concern repeatedly. Each child needs to be treated as an individual and to have the experience of adults recognising and ideally enjoying this individuality. This can be done in everyday ways, such as workers sharing a special joke with a child; remembering birthdays and important occasions; remembering a child's favourite food and so on.

The issue of consistency and reliability in workers' relationships with children is problematic in many Social Services Departments which experience difficulties in the retention of staff. Rapid staff turnover undoubtedly effects the quality of listening to children that is achieved in many local authority settings.

When starting to listen to children, it is important to address the issue of confidentiality with the child, parent or other carer. Local authority workers cannot offer complete confidentiality of information and need to state this. Firstly most workers work within a managerial hierarchy where they are expected to discuss their work with supervisors. Secondly the statutory function means that a worker must act on information that gives cause for concern about a child's welfare. Thirdly it will generally be the case that a worker will want to work in a context where information is shared with a parent or carer. This does not mean that everything a child says has to be relayed to a parent or a carer, but some things need to be placed with the adult who has the day to day care of the child. A child or young person can be offered a degree of privacy in the work so that she/he can express strong emotions about their situation, but a worker needs to identify with a child those feelings that need to be said openly to the family or carer and to support a child to do this.

Many children with whom social workers have contact find it hard to put feelings into words. They will instead 'act out' conscious and unconscious feelings in their behaviour. Such 'acting out' can take the form of temper tantrums, aggression, running away, sexualised behaviour or self-harm and risk-taking. In these circumstances, workers have to set boundaries and limits to the behaviour, but also to try to understand the feelings and dynamics that underlie the actions. It can be very helpful to a child for a worker to name and acknowledge these feelings. A group of children in the care of an Inner London Borough placed this clearly on the agenda at a meeting held to discuss their views on the care they receive. They stated that they needed their carers not only to control their outbursts of temper, but to understand them as well.

There follows an exploration of a number of different ways in which workers can facilitate communication with children. It is not exhaustive. It is possible to use many of these techniques with families as well as with children. Some types of work discussed have special relevance to particular social work settings.

Play

Montaigne wrote: 'Children's playing are not sports and should be deemed their most serious actions.'[3]

Playing is an activity important in the physical, emotional, educational and social development of all children. From the earliest play of a baby in its parent's arms to engagement in competitive team games, play enables a child to discover and explore his/her body and physical powers; to learn about the world practically and intellectually and to develop their social interactions.

Play also has an important role in the child's emotional maturation. Creative playing is a means of expression for the child's conscious and unconscious inner world. In play, a child can express feelings which he/she cannot put into words or those which he/she experiences as overwhelming. He/she can play out problems in living and may become able to cope with them in a step-by-step process. It is a tool for preparing for the future, enabling the child to experiment with potential adult roles.

Play can be a powerful means of engagement, assessment and therapeutic intervention with children and young people. In social work practice, play can be used at a variety of different levels. Engaging in play may be the way that a worker begins to build a relationship with a child. Observations of a child playing alone or in a peer group will be informative of the child's level of development and social skills, and give an indication of the child's concerns and pre-occupations. Children bring to play both reflections of their daily living experiences and their conscious and unconscious feelings.

In play, children may reveal things about their home lives. For example, children who live in chaotic, violent households without clear boundaries often reflect this in their play. A child's play may raise issues of concern for further assessment and exploration. A child's fantasy play needs to be accepted as such and social workers and others have to reflect carefully on its meaning, taking into account the child's social context and stated concerns and wishes. It is important neither to jump to conclusions nor to deny the significance of child's play.

Play materials can be used by social workers as a medium for communication with children. It will often be easier for a child to communicate information in a representational way using toys, rather than in words. For example, a child can use dolls to show who is in their family and to indicate how close or distant they feel to family members. In the disclosure of sexual abuse, anatomically correct dolls are frequently employed to allow the child to demonstrate and describe the nature and extent of abuse. In both instances, the child can use the materials not only to give information, but also to express emotions about abuse or family relationships.

Social workers can use children's free play as a way of listening to the child's worries, fears and feelings and as a therapeutic tool to enable children to resolve real life worries and internal conflicts. Therapeutic work can be both of a long and short-term nature, task-directed or non-directive in style. Teenagers as well as younger children can use the medium of play to communicate. Therapeutic work must always be structured to be regular and consistent and all concerned, including worker, parent/carer and child need to understand and agree to the work.[4]

In play, children will open up areas of feeling they may not be able to put into words or would deny in conversation. Two examples of my own practice illustrate this. In both circumstances, the communicating took place in a room designated for play/talking and in the context of sessions provided on a weekly basis for a short-term period.

The first case involved a six-year-old boy, whose mother had died when he was three years old. He talked frequently about death, in a general sense, remarking on graveyards and asking workers if they believed in heaven. In his play, he chose to set up a situation where he and I made paper flowers, which he laid on a pretend grave for his mother in the sandtray. The sadness and intensity of his feelings was evident as he mourned his mother in play.

In the second situation, a fourteen-year-old girl was confronting the terminal illness of a parent. While at many levels she could use words to talk about her feelings, it was only in play she could express those that overwhelmed her or were too painful or unacceptable to directly address. By using a doll to represent herself, she could explore her sense of guilt for her mother's illness and her fears that she would share a similar fate to her mother. In conversation she would have denied such feelings.

If social workers wish to use play as a means of communication they need to consider the provision of time, space, resources and the development of practice skills. In some Social Service provision, such as day nurseries, play materials are routinely available. In others, such as field work offices and residential homes for adolescents, attention is rarely given to play as a means of communication.

Children's homes, family centres and field work offices can benefit from the setting up of rooms that are designed to enable direct work and play work with children. A vast array of material can be bewildering to a child and a small amount of well-chosen material will best equip such a room. It is useful to have media, such as paints, clay, sand and water tray and dolls' house, that enable free play. Some children will be too inhibited to use such materials, and so structured games for child and adult to play can have value. It is essential that play materials are relevant to the racial and cultural backgrounds of children.

Workers who are thinking of using play or art for the first time as a means of communication with children, often experience apprehension. Most workers are experienced at verbal communication. In presenting play as a means of communication they fear the child's rejection of the medium. Children do not in general share the worker's inhibitions. Workers also fear that they will not know how to understand or deal with what the child presents. Workers who undertake therapeutic work with children need access to consultation and supervision so that they can develop practice skills in listening to children via play and to learn to stay with the intensity of emotions that children play out.

Pens, paper and paints

For children and adults, pens and paper may be an easier way of communicating than talking, whether this is in drawing or writing. Children can find it useful to write down their worries, wishes and questions. They may find it useful to prepare for an important meeting in their lives, such as a review meeting for a child looked after by the local authority, by writing down their agenda of important items and their wishes and feelings. Children will sometimes choose or can be encouraged to write down things they cannot say directly in letter or note form.

Painting and drawing can be used, like play, in a variety of ways from the free expression of emotion in a painting to tasks that are structured as a tool for the communication of information and the exploration of feelings.

In work with families and individual children, a powerful tool in understanding a child's world view is that of drawing with the child/family a family tree. For an older child, such an exercise may produce a diagram like a family genogram. For a younger child, it may be that a pictorial representation of a tree may better hook the child's imagination. In each case, the pictorial representation opens avenues for exploring the child's feelings about people and events in their family lives. It is striking how this exercise can broaden the scope of both the worker's and the child's thinking about the family. A child may introduce as significant someone on whom the worker has not placed importance: for instance a dead grandparent, a former carer or even a pet. The worker may be able to discuss with an older child new perceptions about relationships and patterns in the family that help to increase a child's understanding.

Exercises that involve children in the pictorial representation of their emotions, wishes or scenes from their lives can be of great value in opening up communication. A few examples include the child drawing happy, sad, surprised faces; depicting themselves and others as animals; drawing a safe or a dangerous place.[5] For many children, it will be important that the adults involved also participate. This often frees the child to explore and use the medium freely.

Social workers can themselves use writing and drawing to communicate information to children for whom they are responsible. For example, children who are looked after by a local authority can benefit from the provision of a Handbook which explains various aspects of being in their situation, such as the law, the role of the child's daily carer, the social worker and the natural family, the child's rights and how they can complain about their care, and so on.

It may sometimes be that workers can better help children to understand their situation in pictures than in words. For example, a child awaiting adoption needs help to understand the complex legal and procedural process that has to be undertaken. A pictorial representation of the stages of adoption may well have more impact for a young child than verbal explanations.

Activity based work

Activity-based work offers a way for workers to build relationships with children and young people who would have no interest in a talking relationship. In addition, engagement in constructive activities can provide a child or young person with a sense of self-esteem and achievement and with new skills.

Activity-based work has been used most frequently in day settings, such as work with young offenders in Intermediate Treatment, and in residential settings. It can include adventure holidays, drama, music, projects involving the repair and racing of motor cars, or the development of individual hobbies, such as horse-riding, swimming and fishing.

The process of engaging a child or young person in an activity that is mutually satisfying to child and adult may be the most important step in enabling a child to build trust and open up communication with adults.

Primary care

In the same way as activity-based work may be the cornerstone of communicating with some children, the provision of good primary care in residential and day settings is the basis on which communica-

5 Active listening

tion with children will rest. Workers and carers who live with children are the best placed to build relationships of trust with children, and they can use daily care both to listen to and to meet the emotional as well as the physical needs of children.

Many children who are looked after by local authorities have experienced deprivation and abuse. They may never have established secure attachments to parents or carers. Children who have had positive parental care can experience separation as bewildering and traumatic.

Many children in residential and foster care exhibit physical and emotional needs characteristic of children younger than their chronological years. Children who experience a major life change often regress in their behaviour and needs. Children who have not experienced good early primary care may, when they feel settled on a residential or foster home, go through a period when they need their regressed needs recognised and met. Examples of regressed needs include a five-year-old who wants to be spoon fed or a fourteen-year-old who needs bed-time stories and cuddly toys. It is useful for workers to remember that a child who presents regressed needs will, when these are sufficiently satisfied, move through the regression and over time develop more age appropriate responses.

The process of daily living offers many opportunities for talking to children. In residential settings, it is important to identify ways in which each child is given quiet time with specific adults, so listening and talking are actively encouraged. Children often use informal times to talk. I have always found, for instance, that car journeys are a constructive time for listening and talking to children.

Children will often exhibit worries, feelings and problems in action and relationships. A child may have severe temper tantrums or exhibit sexualised behaviour. Workers need to control and educate children about appropriate behaviour. Many children who have been sexually abused require discussion and demonstration of appropriate physical boundaries, as well as therapeutic help to come to terms with their feelings about the abuse.

Children on a conscious and unconscious level will seek to re-create earlier patterns of relationship with present carers. Carers can find themselves angry or feel helpless, despairing or in conflict with one another, in the process of looking after children. If workers are given help to reflect on the emotional process that caring for particular children produces, they are able to listen at a very deep level to the emotional life of the children in their care.

Life story books

One method for working with children in the long-term care of

Local Authorities is the life story book. It is a tool commonly used in working with children who are to be placed in adoptive and long-term foster families. It is useful, however, in work with all children in local authority care and with children who are with their natural families, but have a history of moves and separations.

The central purpose of the book is to provide the child with a record of his/her background and identity, including information about natural parents and an explanation of separations and moves. It may contain photographs, writing, drawings, birth certificate, and family tree.

With babies and young infants, a worker will usually complete the book on a child's behalf. Once a child is at an age to understand, involvement in the compiling of the book can be a powerful therapeutic tool. The child and worker can together find out facts and information about the child's life, visit former carers, schools and so on.

The life story book provides a focus for the child to achieve an understanding of their past and to work through feelings about it. Workers often have to set aside the completion of the book as the focus of work, while the child explores emotions about the past.

It is useful for the book to be compiled in a loose-leaf folder so that the child can add to and re-arrange sections over time. The book usually comes to hold great emotional significance for the child and may be the vehicle through which the child chooses to introduce him/her self to a new family.

The involvement of natural parents in the compilation of life story books, in terms of the provision of information about the child's life and family background is important. Natural parents often take great time and attention in providing such information. Sometimes they use this to continue to work through their own feelings of loss. It is also a way in which they make a positive contribution to their child's future.

Group work

Many children will not easily talk in a one to one situation with an adult, and find it possible to communicate more freely in a group setting. Children and young people will sometimes request that they meet other people who share the same life experiences as themselves, so they can compare and learn from each others' experiences. For example, survivors of sexual abuse can gain much from groups that enable them to discuss their experiences and feelings together. Groups also provide a forum for children to develop social skills and to form friendships. Just as in individual work, communication in groups can be facilitated in a wide range of ways.

One of the key functions of a group is to reduce isolation and a group for abuse survivors can also help to lessen the victim's inevitable guilt feelings. Children can see that others were not to blame for their own abuse and so can eventually realise that they need not blame themselves either. A child's self esteem is raised as she learns to help others to cope with experience.

Talking

When talking to children, it is useful to bear in mind some simple and general principles that facilitate rather than close down communication. Firstly, it is important that an adult demonstrates an interest in the child and their world, establishing rapport with the child about things that have his/her attention. This may involve talking to a young child about a toy or to an older child about school or hobbies.

A worker needs to think about coming to the child's level in order to communicate. This may involve physically moving to the child's level and using words and language that a child understands. It is helpful to note and use the child's vocabulary. For instance, in sexual abuse disclosure work, it is important to check out and use a child's words for sexual organs.

Asking a child, or indeed an adult, questions that can be answered with a 'Yes' or a 'No' can lead to closed and unproductive communication. It is worth practising how to ask open-ended questions.

In the field of Family Therapy, the Milan School of therapists have developed a style of family interviewing based on a technique called 'Circular Questioning'.[6] The technique is designed to focus on differences between family members and on change. It is possible to adapt and use some of the technique in work with individual children and adults.

The technique can be used in a variety of ways. The worker asks one family member to comment on the relationship between two other family members. For example, a child could be asked about the relationship between a parent and another sibling in the family or about an event in the family which did not directly involve him or her. Questions are asked where the child is asked to rank differences between family members. For example, a child in local authority accommodation can be asked who in his/her family shows most and least concern about the child's separation from the family.

The child can also be asked to talk about how other members of the family view an event. Questions can also be directed to looking at changes over time: for example, a child can be asked whether his mother was more or less strict before his father left the family.

Questions can be raised about the future: for example, a child can be asked if their parent would be more or less angry, if a particular event were to happen in the future.

'Circular Questioning' thus provides a number of different ways of asking open-ended questions. The questions can in themselves lead a child or family to recognise differences, connections and changes that have gone unnoticed.

Important verbal communication can often take place with children by way of metaphor and story telling. It has been my experience in working with children that they frequently recount film or television scripts as a way of talking about their own experiences. Children separated from their families often use stories of separation and reunion to explore their own feelings and wishes. Sometimes children can make or appreciate the connection between their own life and the fictional story. Often, however, interpretations made by workers of connections will fall on deaf ears, but long conversations about feelings can be held when talking about these fictional characters. Metaphor and story are powerful ways to communicate and workers can employ them to notable effect to communicate a message to a child or a family.

Non-verbal communication

In all human communication there are frequent contradictions between what people say and their non-verbal communication. It is important to notice these contradictions when working with children. A child's non-verbal communication may be a powerful indicator of stress or distress. A young child who flinches involuntarily at the approach of a parent may be giving important information about their home situation.

The emotional impact of listening to children

Listening to children who are dealing with issues of abuse or separation from family is very emotionally demanding. Unless workers are prepared to listen to and tolerate children's painful feelings, such as anger, guilt, desperation, worthlessness and rejection, a worker will not enable the child to communicate.

Working with children in such situations can trigger for all workers feelings about their own experiences. Social workers who are not able to confront painful emotions in their past and present life will not be able to work effectively at a deep level. Workers need to recognise when their own feelings are blocking communication with children. There are times when workers can legitimately feel that particular pieces of work touch them too personally for them to work effectively. Managers need to respect this in the allocation of work.

The experience of allowing children to express strong emotions can be exhausting, painful and even frightening. Listening to children is equally one of the most rewarding and educative professional experiences.

An example that characterised this in my own practice was working with a teenager placed in residential care. She had regular play sessions and in one of these, she modelled clay to represent human figures. She then stuck pins systematically into these 'dolls' as a torture. She finally destroyed them with heart-felt aggression.

At the time, I and my co-worker were disturbed and perplexed by her actions. In consultation with colleagues, we came to understand the meaning of her actions. She had been waiting for a foster family for two years and no family had come forward for her. She was using the clay 'dolls' to represent her own feelings of being tortured by this wait. In the next session, we talked to her of our understanding. She agreed with our interpretation and talked of her feelings. She had felt rejected by her family of origin and now felt rejected again as no foster family wanted her. We explored her feelings of anger towards ourselves as people connected with the failure to find her a family.

It is a piece of communication that not only had relevance to the work with the particular young person and our relationship with her, but it presents a graphic picture of the feelings that can be generated by a long wait for family placement. It provides a challenge to the practice and policy-making of many Social Services Departments.

Listening to children is a complex and demanding task. Workers require access to training, consultation and supervision, if they are to listen effectively. They need to work in a framework that supports and encourages them to acknowledge and work with children's painful emotions. They will need time and the help of colleagues and consultants to reflect on the meaning of a child's communication and on how to use that understanding to the benefit of the child.

References

1. *A Child in Trust: The Report of the panel of inquiry into the circumstances surrounding the death of Jasmine Beckford* (1985) London Borough of Brent.
2. *Children Act 1989* (1989) HMSO.
3. Montaigne, (c1563) *Essays I xxiii*, M. Rats 1959 edn,
4. Axline, Virginia M. (1989) *Play Therapy*, Churchill Livingstone.
5. Oaklander, Violet (1978) *Windows to our Chidren*, Real People Press.
6. Palazzoli, M. S., Cecchim G., Prata G. and Boscola L. (1980) 'Hypothesizing, circularity and neutrality: three guidelines for the conductor of the session', *Family Process* .

6 A permanent mark? — management responsibility in child protection work

Murray Davies

And the first step, as you know, is always what matters most, particularly when we are dealing with those who are young and tender. That is the time when they are taking shape, and when any impression we choose to make leaves a permanent mark.[1]

There is a danger in that looking to the welfare of the children, believed to be victims of sexual abuse, the children themselves may be overlooked. The child is a person, and not an object of concern. Professionals should always listen carefully to what the child has to say, and to take seriously what is said.[2]

When a court determines any question with respect to:
(a) the upbringing of a child; or
(b) the administration of a child's property or the application of any incoming arising from it,
the child's welfare shall be the court's paramount consideration.[3]

And so we are reminded of the importance and the need to afford respect to the child — to consider the rights of children. Children have rights of their own, independent of their parents, in particular the right to grow and develop with their basic needs satisfied and free from harm and abuse. This principle was voiced by the NSPCC in 1988 in their campaign asking parents and *professionals* to reconsider how they treat children and to ask them to put children first.

6 A permanent mark

In this chapter I argue that individual professionals who work directly with abused children and their families must have their own needs met if they are to continue to survive and work in this difficult field. I describe the consequences of the failure to meet the needs of such staff and outline the components of good individual supervision provided by first line managers. I examine the need for healthy organisations and the role and skills required of managers to produce them if a high quality service is to be provided to some of the least powerful members of our society. Finally, I describe how behaviour is mirrored from our organisations to the families we work with and from families back to professionals. In individual, team, organisational and multi-disciplinary settings the need to understand the other's world from his point of view is the key to good communication and relationships. Without such support the ability of the most skilled professional to engage in listening to children will inevitably diminish over time. Managers have a key responsibility to prevent this from happening.

The welfare net

A wide range of agencies and professional workers are concerned with the welfare of children: social workers have a major role in investigating, assessing and arranging for the treatment of child abuse; community nursing services, in particular health visitors, have a recognised concern for young children and those at risk; family doctors have the advantage of knowing families over a long period of time and may often be the first to know when someone's situation or circumstances change and arouse concern. Teachers can develop very close relationships with children, and be aware of significant events in their lives; the police have community responsibilities, are often turned to at moments of domestic crisis and have particular responsibilities in protecting children from harm.

With the increased awareness of child abuse in its many forms, it is important that those working for the welfare of children are trained and organised to be sensitive and alert to the needs of children. It is important to make time for children, to respect them, to listen to them and to be sensitive to their capacities to understand what is being asked of them. There is now a climate of concern about child abuse, good child care and what to do for the best.

Professional responsibilities

So what is required of organisations, and what can go wrong?

Children tell us about their feelings and thoughts in a variety of ways, and very young children may not have the words to express what has happened. Instead, they may act in certain ways, giving early warning signs that something is wrong and they need help. Listening is very important. Organisations have responsibilities to ensure that their staff have the skills to listen, and are properly supported and encouraged in this task. Active listening involves listening carefully to what the child says. Not questioning, not giving advice, not lecturing, not smoothing over and not demanding — just listening. Active listening is an important way of showing the child that you are interested in their point of view.

At times words do not tell the whole story. The child may not even know his or her own feelings. Listening for feelings and trying to show understanding is important. 'You seem worried about..., you sound very disappointed...' When communicating with the children, the skill is to enter a child's world and to view the problem from a child's frame of reference, i.e. to understand what the child is feeling about whom. It is impossible to work with children without making effective use of media other than words in order to enter their world and empathise with their predicament. Children may need permission to have feelings, even when they seem to be denying them. Abused children can demonstrate very destructive behaviour towards themselves and towards others and this behaviour may be seen as an attempt to solve a problem rather than be one. It becomes important to listen to what is not being expressed, or what is being avoided, to the anxieties and the fears.

Personal difficulties

Skills in communicating with children are of paramount importance to all of those in contact with children, and working to promote their welfare. It is vital to ensure that staff are equipped to listen to children, and that their receptiveness is maintained. Experiencing the pain of children, especially children who have been abused, can be very difficult to bear and to contemplate. Personal experience, which underlies all professional behaviour, may resonate, bringing back painful past experiences and feelings, such as abuse and anger and producing confusion or paralysis in current roles and responsibilities. Fantasies also may be evoked, regardless of personal realities, when dealing with the results of physical, sexual or emotional abuse of children. Denial that parents can and do injure their children may occur from the continuous bombardment of distressing cases. Such emotional responses to abuse and the feelings aroused may not have an outlet. These unexpressed feelings may impede the appropriate use of procedures, statutory responsibilities and the acceptance of accountability. It is often easier not to acknowledge such feelings, and so deny one's own vulnerability. Under such circumstances the ability to help others to confront emotional responses to abuse is seriously limited.

Staff care

Staff from different professional backgrounds and in different organisational settings, who encounter the pain and suffering of children and adults, bear the immediate distress. If such staff are to be effective in the delivery of their skills and services, they need proper care and attention provided to them by the organisation and by its managers. A commitment to quality services, by any organisation, requires a commitment to the care and support of the human resource. In the welfare field the human resource is critical to the delivery and provision of services. Staff who have the ability and the preparedness to encounter the pain of others are essential if those in need are to have an opportunity to resolve the impact of earlier abusive experiences on them.

Individuals working alone with child-abusing families may be at risk from the precarious combination of professional responsibility and isolation. Burn out may become a consequence for the individual:

> Burn out involves the loss of concern for the people with whom one is working. In addition to physical exhaustion (and sometimes even illness), burn out is characterised by an emotional exhaustion in which the professional no longer has any positive feelings, sympathy or respect for clients and patients. A very cynical and dehumanised perception of these people often develops in which they are labelled in derogatory ways and treated accordingly. As a result of this dehumanising process these people are viewed as somehow deserving of their problems and are blamed for their own victimisation and, thus, there is a deterioration in the quality of care service that they receive...The professional who burns out is unable to cope successfully with the overwhelming stresses of the job and this failure to cope can be manifested in a number of ways, ranging from impaired performance and absenteeism to various types of personal problems, such as alcohol and drug abuse, marital conflict and mental illness. People who burn out often quit their jobs or even change professions whilst some seek psychiatric treatment for what they believe to be their personal failings.[4]

Dealing with abused children and their families can be particularly demanding of staff. 'Work with abusing families is exhausting and threatening; seldom immediately, and sometimes never rewarding. In this context it is vital for practitioners not to neglect their own needs regarding emotional balance and survival.'[5]

The high price of burn out has also been commented on. 'Clients are treated badly, dehumanised and poorly served. Communities are robbed of effective public services.'[6]

Staff care then is vital and managers must be aware of the emotional and physical health of their staff. Burnt out practitioners will not be able to respond sensitively to children or adults, will be unable to communicate with them and may distance themselves from any emotional involvement. The same may be true of managers, and if those responsible for organising staff within an organisation cannot care for them, how can practitioners care for those in need? Small teams can offer benefits to staff, providing an emotional reservoir for members to draw on.

> Whilst this may filter an important degree of professional stress away from the practitioner's own family, and be beneficial for that reason, perhaps more importantly it diminishes the tendency for workers under stress to turn to their clients for covert personal support. Having a firm base in a team can go a long way to helping practitioners to avoid the situation of needing to get more help from their client families than families can get from them.[7]

Supervision

The report of the Inquiry into the circumstances surrounding the death of Jasmine Beckford, *A Child In Trust*, recommended: 'the practice of planning regular discussions between health visitors and their senior nurses should be established, and senior nurses should particularly ensure that they discuss all child abuse cases regularly with the health visitor involved even if she herself does not consider that there is any problem with which she is unable to deal'.

Some disciplines do not have formal supervisory arrangements, which allow a practitioner's practice to be focused on, questioned and checked. However, no matter how experienced an individual practitioner, it is not always easy to disentangle oneself from the demands and pressures of everyday practice. The Cleveland inquiry highlighted this dilemma in respect of paediatricians:

> ...it was entirely proper for the two paediatricians to play their part in the identification of sexual abuse in children referred to them. They were responsible for the care of their patients. Non-the-less they had a responsibility to examine their own actions;

to consider whether their practice was always correct and whether it was in the best interests of the children and their patients. They are to be criticised for not doing so and for the certainty and over-confidence with which they pursued the detection of sexual abuse in children referred to them.[8]

The Cleveland inquiry also drew attention to the importance of supervision in one of its recommendations. 'Staff engaged in social work practice in the field of child abuse and child sexual abuse need structured arrangements for their supervision and personal support. The work is stressful and it is important that their personal needs are not overlooked.'[9]

Care of staff is critical, and the role of the supervisor essential and crucial in this process. The requirements and characteristics of the 'ideal supervisor' were highlighted in the training video tape and guide *Acceptable Risk*:

> Supervisors should be able to give advice, help with ongoing learning, know how to work the system, be supportive in relation to senior management and be able to pick up the frustrations of social workers with regard to resources, stress and emergencies, and be able to offer praise and encouragement. They should be available and aware of their supervisees as individuals as well as professionals, being sensitive to feelings, though not intervening inappropriately in personal lives.[10]

The supervisory relationship is concerned with respect for the individual practitioner, listening to his or her needs and responding to these. If an individual practitioner feels that his or her needs are being met in their role, that they are motivated in their practice and are equipped to meet the needs of others, then they are more likely to respond by listening to the needs of others, whether they are children or parents. As with children, so with practitioners; if needs are being met practitioners are more likely to attend to the needs of others. If needs are being frustrated, energy is more likely to be diverted into seeking satisfaction of personal needs, maybe by battling with the organisation or colleagues and having little energy or motivation to attend to the needs of others. Staff care is critical if staff in turn are to care for their clients: children and adults.

Managers must not be excluded from the process; they also have needs. Supervisors, who are often first-line managers, also require support and supervision. When they are respected and listened to, if their needs are understood and responded to, then they are more likely to respond in this way to their supervisees, and so good practice develops. If supervisors and their managers fail to listen to feelings, fail to respect their human resources, and plan and operate more mechanistic bureaucratic services, they fail to respect individual needs.

Providing quality service

If, as managers, we fail to pay attention to the needs of individuals, it is impossible to provide a quality service. Quality is simply 'the meeting of the customer's requirements', and is not restricted to the functional characteristics of products or services. In short, if we are not listening to the needs of our customers, children and parents, we are not providing quality services.

John Oakland offers the following illustration of quality:

'Is this a quality watch?'

The answers vary:

'No it's made in Japan.'
'No it's cheap.'
'No the face is scratched.'
'How reliable is it?'
'I wouldn't wear it.'

Very rarely am I told that the quality of the watch depends upon what the wearer requires from a watch — a piece of jewellery to give an impression of wealth, or a time piece which gives the required data, including the date, in digital form. Clearly these requirements determine the quality.

Quality is often used to signify 'excellence' of a product or service — we talk about Rolls Royce quality, and top quality. If we are to define quality in a way which is useful in its management, then we must recognise the need to include in the assessment of quality, the true requirement of 'the customer'.[11]

To achieve quality we must listen.

There are also customers within organisations. A range of staff perform different functions, have needs and requirements of each other. Do they meet each other's requirements? Do others — our colleagues, managers, supervisors? Are the roles of others in the organisation respected, and is the vital importance of all the different contributions recognised?

Failure to meet requirements in any part of the organisation has a way of multiplying, and failure in one part of the system creates problems elsewhere, leading to yet more failure, more problems and so on. The price of quality is the continual examination of the requirements and the ability to meet them.

Organisational patterns

Listening to children, then, is not an isolated process, but is an important organisational pattern. A key question for everyone to ask is 'Are my requirements being met?' This is a key measure of whether individuals are being listened to. The process of listening, or not listening, mirrors itself up and down organisations, and out into the community, to the children who need to be listened to. Talking and listening to children is not an isolated process that takes place between the social worker and the child, the teacher and the child, even the policeman and the child. Talking and listening describe the process of a healthy organisation. If the organisation is healthy, it is more likely to be able to promote the health of others.

Active listening

Active listening is contagious. If people complain that they are never listened to, the chances are that they don't listen.

Active listening can promote a feeling of warmth between people. The experience of being heard and understood satisfies and creates feelings of warmth towards the listener. When someone listens deeply, they get to understand, to empathise with and to become the other person.

Active listening is an important part of the process of demonstrating respect to other people. Respect is one of the three fundamental skills to making effective relationships. The other two skills are genuineness and empathy. Respect describes behaviour which conveys to others that they are worthwhile, unique and valuable — helping someone feel that they are important.

Genuineness is behaviour which conveys to others that you are real, appropriately open about yourself, and not hiding behind a role or façade.

Empathy is behaviour which shows an understanding of the other person's world as they are experiencing it. Such behaviour within organisations enables effective relationships to develop and makes the development of effective relationships outside, with children, with parents, and with professional colleagues, more likely.

Managers

> Research has shown that a manager's job consists mostly of interpersonal transactions; senior managers spend up to 80% of their time in oral communication with their superiors, col-

leagues, subordinates and people inside and outside their work unit, and really half of a manager's time is spent generating information. Thus the importance of developing skills in interpersonal interactions is obvious. Managing relationships forms the greater part of a manager's job.[12]

In order to ensure that interpersonal communication is well managed, two simultaneously occurring aspects must be addressed: passing information and building relationships. Miscommunication can take place by simply concentrating on use of language. Personal values, beliefs, assumptions and perceptions can distort the effectiveness of inter-personal communication.

Kakabadse draws on the work of Karl Albrecht to describe four means of communication:

> *Facts* are objective reality, or inferences, assumptions believed to be true on the basis of our previous experience.
>
> *Feelings* are our emotional responses to this situation in relation to our previous experience; our reactions to the context and content of this transaction.
>
> *Values* are the norms of behaviour which we feel are appropriate for use within our society and culture; reasonably permanent beliefs about what should or should not be important for us.
>
> *Opinions* are attitudes which are relevant to the particular position one has taken in this transaction; short term beliefs about this situation which are subjective not objective reality.
>
> All four of these channels are used in any interaction...and problems of miscommunication occur when messages sent on one channel are thought to be sent on another, for example an opinion is received and interpreted as a fact.[13]

To reduce these misperceptions, and avoid consequent frustration and anger, all practitioners, and their supervisors and managers need to be aware that a message consists not just of content (the apparent facts), but also of the underlying feelings, values, and opinions of the sender. It is important to listen actively to messages and to reflect back the expressed content and feelings to be sure the whole message is received and understood.

Organisations

Organisations exist to achieve certain objectives, purposes or goals, and develop strategies, policies and plans for achieving these objectives. Structure provides the mechanism through which strategies can be implemented. Structure involves establishing role hierarchies, introducing controls and appropriate information and administrative systems and using necessary resources. The two key resources in any organisation are money and people. The former is required to finance the organisation, and organisations need people to get things done. Those managing the organisation can only get their work done through the human resource in the organisation. Skills with people, being able to develop open and trusting relationships, to listen and collaborate, to create climates within which people are self-motivated, are crucial. Understanding why people behave as they do, and, for practitioners and managers, the likely consequences of their own behaviour is essential.

Wherever staff are employed within an organisation, the groups with whom the individual interacts also influence their performance at work. Groups satisfy various functions, ranging from formal groups whose purpose is to achieve particular tasks or goals, to informal groups which can fulfil both professional and social needs.

Tensions may occur between individuals when personal needs are not being satisfied, and this can lead to anxiety, and stress. When people feel they are not being understood, this may manifest itself in anger, passive or active resistance, defensive behaviour or withdrawal from the situation. Tension can be reduced by attempting to understand the other person's feelings about a situation from his or her point of view. To do this it is important to listen actively and with empathy to the other person to reduce any threat and to show understanding and acceptance. The motives for another person's behaviour become clearer when shared. Tensions between individuals can be reduced by managers developing knowledge and skills to manage inter-personal transactions, and to avoid breakdowns in communication.

Andrew Kakabadse draws attention to the skills managers require to manage interpersonal relationships, to work well with other people and to be able to lead a group successfully, this

> ...means being able to develop the skills of diagnosis and analysis of interpersonal situations, and also the skills of effective communication. The skills of diagnosis and analysis should not be seen as just thinking skills. They need to be recognised as natural, thinking and feeling, everyday skills. Looking at the situation and the impact of communication from the other's point of view at least ensures sufficient sensitivity to allow a meaningful discourse between two people. You do not have to 'take on board' the other person's point of view, but just appreciate that your impact on them affects their communication with you.[9]

Professional networks

Children and families exist within a network of professionals and agencies. When children are abused, no single discipline has all the knowledge and skills necessary to diagnose effectively, and to provide remedial services. Professionals need to work together, sharing their areas of expertise, and listening to each other. Inquiries into fatal cases have highlighted shortcomings in communication and collaboration between agencies. Failings in inter-personal communication can have profound, and tragic consequences for children. Similar findings and concerns were voiced in the Cleveland enquiry.

> The problems of child sexual abuse have been recognised to an increasing extent over the past few years by professionals of different disciplines. This presents new and particularly difficult problems for the agencies concerned in child protection. In Cleveland an honest attempt was made to address these problems by the agency: in Spring 1987 it went wrong.
>
> The reasons for the crisis are complex. In essence they included:
>
> Lack of a proper understanding by the main agencies of each other's functions in relation to child sexual abuse;
>
> A lack of communication between the agencies;
>
> Differences of views at middle management level which were not recognised by senior staff. These eventually affected those working on the ground.[2]

Relationship problems occur within families, within organisations, and when organisations attempt to work together. Inter-agency working has been formally encouraged since the DHSS circular in 1974, 'a case conference is recommended for every case involving suspected non-accidental injury to a child. In this way, unilateral action will be minimised, and all those who can provide information about the child and his family, have statutory responsibility for the safety of the child, or are responsible for providing services will be brought together to reach a collective decision.'[15]

This circular followed the tragic death of Maria Colwell which highlighted the importance of practitioners talking to each other. 'Maria fell through the welfare net...primarily because of communications failures.'[16]

Perhaps the most dangerous aspect of inter-agency functioning lies in the ways in which agencies relate to one another, which can reflect the same patterns of behaviour as normal and abnormal families. 'There are healthy conflicts and rivalries; clear and blurred boundaries; alliances and scapegoats; overt and covert communication patterns and the operation of supportive, provocative and even destructive patterns of behaviour.'[17] At times difficulties in relationships between professionals from different disciplines can affect and seriously interfere with responses to individual children.

Professionals working together will have different backgrounds in training, and possibly different objectives in their role. The police, for example, may be concerned about culpability in respect of a criminal offence, whereas a social worker may be seeking an understanding of the causes of the abuse, in order to consider a possible remedial action. A doctor may be concerned only with the treatment of particular injuries. A common thread for different professionals is a general concern for the child in the family, and the need to prevent further abuse of the child. The more that different professionals can listen to each other, understand each other's viewpoint expressed in a jargon-free understandable way, the more likely it is that services to children will improve. Working together calls for respect for all professional colleagues, whatever their discipline, and whatever their status. It is important to recognise and respect all contributions. This mirrors the respect shown to contributions from the child. Staff working in schools, or other day or residential settings, have contributions as vital as the consultant paediatrician or the area social services manager. Sometimes communication becomes blocked because individuals need, and cling onto, the status ascribed to their role. If by speaking from roles, and hierarchical positions, the views of others are not listened to, respected and recognised, communication is seriously impaired, and information is lacking.

Mirroring families

Practitioners individually and collectively are affected by children and the families with whom they work, and multi-disciplinary groups, for example core groups managing child protection cases, can begin to mirror processes within families. If conflict in families is avoided, this may be repeated in the professional group or, conversely, there may be conflict within families, with different professionals unconsciously being drawn into alliances with family members and repeating conflicts with professional colleagues. Practitioners may experience themselves fighting the family battles for them by proxy. Colleagues working with an abuser may find themselves rejected by the professional network, mirroring the behaviour of the family.

It is not always easy, but all have a responsibility to identify such processes, and make them overt. In such a way, further information is obtained about the dynamics of life in the family, and the potential for change. If the professional network is stuck in particular patterns of behaviour, repeating conflicts, isolating individual members, there is little possibility of the family changing. If the professional network cannot work on resolving these problems, it can offer little for the child. It merely confirms and maintains possible destructive dynamics, and limits the solutions and new experiences which could be developed for children and their families.

Improving relationships

Conflicts, tensions, difficulties with individuals or groups in organisations are inevitable. People have their own views on issues, their own approaches to solving problems. Conflict between individuals and within groups can arise because of disagreement on particular issues or because of the manner in which discussions took place.

Andrew Kakabadse recommends the following approaches to achieve greater collaboration and commitment amongst people:

1. *Reflective listening* both improves understanding of common problems and generates sufficient trust between individuals for them to talk to each other.

2. *Assertion Skills* make a powerful impact on people and also maintain their commitment to working in the organisation.

   Assertiveness is the mid-point between submissive and aggressive behaviours and is about being clear and firm whilst being responsive to the other person.

3. *Fewer Communication Blocks* between individuals can be achieved by reducing dominating, threatening and aggressive behaviour and making fewer false judgements.

4. *Issues*, rather than just inter-personal tensions, should be emphasised. This means gathering facts, breaking larger issues into smaller workable units, and then confronting each problem spearately.

5. *Careful Appraisal of the Actions Decided* and an assessment of the consequences of those actions is a valuable discipline to undertake, for it may deter both individuals and groups from needless disputes in the future.[18]

Effective problem solving is achieved through sharing information, obtaining commitment from others and involving others in the decision-making process.

There are many similarities in the process of problem solving within organisations, and in the multi-disciplinary context with the process of helping children and families resolve problems.

The importance of listening

Whatever the setting, problems need to be properly understood before solutions can be derived. Problems can only be understood, and tensions reduced, by really attempting to understand the other person's feelings about a situation from their point of view. This can only be done by listening actively, and with empathy to the other person, to reduce any threat and to show understanding and acceptance.

If we are to listen to others, we need to feel that we are listened to ourselves, that we are respected and valued. If we feel valued, we are more likely to value others. If we feel listened to, we are more likely to offer this experience to others.

Managers at all levels in organisations have a responsibility to ensure that their staff are in touch with those to whom they provide services. To be in touch, means to listen and to talk — to communicate. The manager's responsibility is not simply to identify 'a good course', and to provide more and more training. If the organisation is not functioning, the most skilled staff will find it difficult to perform. They may feel dissatisied, their performance may decline, and they may leave. *The manager's responsibility is to practise listening skills.*

If we all carefully listen to professional colleagues in our own and other disciplines, if we all listen to our managers and to those for whom we are responsible, the way in which we serve the needs of children will improve immeasurably.

References

1. Plato, *The Republic*. Penguin Classics 1955.
2. *Report of the Inquiry into Child Abuse in Cleveland 1987* (1988) HMSO.
3. *Children Act 1989*, HMSO.
4. Maslach, C. and Pines, A. 'The Burn Out Syndrome in the Day Care Setting', *Child Care Quarterly* (6, 1977).
5. Dale P., Davies M. *et al. Dangerous Families. Assessment and Treatment of Child Abuse.* (1986) Tavistock Publications.
6. Armstrong K. 'Burnout' *Caring* (7, 2, 1981).
7. Dale, Davies, *et al.* (1986), *op. cit.*
8. Report of Inquiry (1987) *op. cit.*
9. *Ibid.*
10. Ash, Elizabeth (1988), *Acceptable Risk. Supervision in Child Abuse Cases.* CCETSW.
11. Oakland, J. *Total Quality Management* (1989) Heinemann.

12. Kakabadse, A., Ludlow, R. and Vinnicombe, S. *Working in Organisations.* (1988) Penguin Business.
13. *Ibid.*
14. Report of Inquiry (1987) *op. cit.*
15. DHSS Circular LASSL (74) 13.
16. *Report of Committee of Inquiry into the Care and Supervision provided in relation to Maria Calwell.* (1974) HMSO.
17. Dale, Davies *et al.* (1986) *op. cit.*
18. Kakabadse *et al.* (1988) *op. cit.*

Part 3
Protecting the abused child: child protection investigation

7 Child abuse investigation — tuning in to the child's world

Eileen Shearer ©

Introduction

The investigation of allegations of child abuse affords social workers a vital opportunity to see and reach out to vulnerable children, and it is essential that we do so with *all* our senses, as well as with our intelligence and emotions. In this chapter, I outline a number of ways in which investigating social workers may be distracted from their task of ensuring the child's safety; I also describe some of the processes which can draw the worker's attention from the child's voice to louder, though possibly less painful sounds in the course of investigations.

Sexual abuse investigations present the most obvious need to listen directly to the child; in many cases the only evidence of abuse will be the child's word. Much attention has been devoted to understanding the dynamics of sexual abuse, and much energy directed to establishing local investigation procedures and joint police and social work training programmes. By contrast, however, the investigation of allegations of physical abuse and neglect has received little attention either in the literature or on training courses. A recent exception is *Journeys into the Unknown* (Erooga, M. and Masson, H. 1990).[1] This stressful, complex and time-consuming social work task is also often professionally and managerially undervalued, with inevitable consequences for the quality of abuse investigation, and occasionally tragic results for children.

7 Child abuse investigation

It is essential to recognise that sexual abuse investigations follow a different pattern from the investigations of physical abuse and neglect. The procedures, process of investigation, and the issues and problems they raise are different in crucial ways. I propose to focus here only on physical abuse and neglect investigations. In these cases, although listening to the child's story is vital, this cannot be the sole focus if the child's situation is to be seen clearly and his protection assured. Listening *is* necessary, but it is by no means sufficient for effective investigation and protection.

Jane's story

Nearly ten years ago, I read a letter written by Jane, a mother who was then attending a Family Centre because of concerns about her abuse of her children. She had a lot of difficulty in bringing them up, and a very stormy, violent marriage. She was articulate, intelligent and painfully aware of her situation.

I have never forgotten her description of her own childhood, when she was persistently beaten and neglected by her alcoholic mother. Although several social workers did investigate allegations of abuse, and some attempted to work 'long-term' with Jane's mother, the abuse continued and the children went unprotected from their mother throughout their childhood.

I was particularly struck by her account for a number of reasons, and the lessons I learned have stayed with me since. Firstly, I felt the pain and tragedy of the situation, both for Jane as a child, and now for her children in turn, thanks to her gift for communication. I was shocked by the skill with which Jane's mother had lied to professionals and presented a plausible front, time after time, as well as by the threats and bribes used to keep the children quiet when social workers asked awkward questions. But Jane's account showed many opportunities for social workers to see through the lies to the truth of the children's plight, and none did so. Perhaps they *had* felt uneasy, but did not know how to translate this feeling into action.

I am convinced of the integrity and genuine concern of those workers, but from Jane's point of view, they failed to see what she needed, or to act on her behalf. To her as a child, it was clear that they seemed gullible, powerless, and easily convinced by her mother's lies.

Secondly, the damage child abuse causes to its victims was powerfully brought home to me, as was the power of parents, who can so easily appeal to our own adult-orientated view of the world, to hide the truth about abuse from workers who investigate such allegations.

Jane's letter also created an emotional shock which started me off on a process of learning so that I would be less likely to miss or ignore the signs of abuse in my own practice. If Jane's experience is multiplied by all the adult clients on our caseloads, how much hitherto unknown abuse would come to light? It seems to me that as social workers concerned with chidren's welfare, we need to base our investigations on the premise that what we see when we investigate, or during our visits to 'long-term cases', is often only a snapshot of the child's experience, and a potentially 'touched up' snapshot at that. Any abuse we do uncover might easily represent only the tip of a large and unpleasant iceberg from the child's point of view.

Child abuse is *not* easy to see; even as social workers we prefer not to believe that parents do such things to their children. Alice Miller (1983)[2] expresses the problem thus:

> We are still barely conscious of how harmful it is to treat children in a degrading manner. Treating them with respect and recognising the consequences of their being humiliated are by no means intellectual matters, otherwise their importance would long since have been generally realised. To empathise with what a child is feeling when he or she is defenceless, hurt or humiliated, is like suddenly seeing in a mirror the suffering of one's own childhood, something many people must ward off out of fear...we ward it off with the aid of illusions such as...believing that children were mistreated in previous centuries or are so in distant countries or cultures.

It is so much easier for professionals to see parents as victims (and, of course, many are) and harder to hold on to the fact that whatever their own damaging experiences as children — no doubt Jane's mother was abused as a child — they still, as parents, have a responsibility to keep their children safe. If they cannot do this, professionals must do so on their behalf and offer them help to change. Investigation is the beginning of this process.

Workers' rights — the foundation of investigations

> Those who undermine the confidence and the morale of the people that society is sending out in its name to protect children should realise they are unwittingly putting children at risk (Louis Blom-Cooper, 1987).[3]

Social workers engaged in child abuse investigation have certain rights without which they will not hear the child's voice clearly, or hold onto it throughout the often difficult process of the investigation.

7 Child abuse investigation

Mandate

Workers are entitled to a clear mandate to undertake investigations of child abuse allegations; yet society's attitude to the detection of child abuse is not straightforward or unambivalent. As Dingwall et al (1983)[4] comment, this results in systems which are 'fully effective neither in preventing mistreatment nor in respecting family privacy, but which lurch unevenly between these two poles.'

The widest mandate to workers and their agencies is enshrined in legislation to protect children; at agency level the mandate is given through clear and specific investigation procedures.

The importance of such agency procedures cannot be overestimated in enabling workers to investigate effectively. Too many agencies still leave their workers uncertain of what is expected of them, and within what time-scale. Clear procedures represent the central point of reference for the worker, and her manager, in the midst of the turmoil and uncertainty of the investigation. They also clarify the shared responsibility for decision-making in the line management structure in cases of child abuse. No worker should take child protection decisions alone; I refer below to the importance of supervision and consultation to ensure safe practice.

In addition to the legal and agency mandates, however, individual workers need to achieve an internal sense of their right to intervene in families' lives. Many social workers lack the confidence to investigate and many do not accept their role as investigators. I recently encountered a colleague waiting to give evidence in Wardship proceedings. Her comment would probably ring true for many social workers: 'I didn't come into social work to do this.' Notions of being helpful to clients, or engaging their trust or helping them to be self-determining, are not easy to reconcile with the investigative role. But it is essential that workers do develop clear child-focused values and become comfortable with the legitimate use of their authority when investigating.

Principles and values

Workers also have the right to work in agencies which have developed clear values and principles in relation to child abuse investigations.

Most fundamental is the principle that children have rights, independent of those of their parents; where the two sets of rights are in conflict, those of the child should prevail.

Thus the investigator's task is to ensure that children, who cannot assert their own rights, have their basic needs met by their caretakers. These include the rights to safety, food, warmth, shelter, security, and loving care. Investigations should also be carried out with attention to the parents' rights to respectful treatment and honesty about our concerns.

The notion that investigation may be a preventive activity is important, yet little recognised. Parents may discuss dificulties (e.g. child management) in the course of an investigation, for which subsequent help can be offered, and the risk of future abuse may thus be diminished.

Abuse investigations should also be based on positive offers of help to all members of the family when abuse or neglect are discovered. This help will focus on enabling parents to change so that they can care for their children safely in the future. On the one hand, the quality of the investigation has a crucial effect on any subsequent therapeutic work; on the other hand, the offer of help is part of the moral basis for investigation.

The current lack of resources for treatment has a serious though covert effect on the willingness of workers to detect abuse. ('She'll be no better off in care.') and on parents to acknowledge it ('She'll be taken off me forever.'). Without treatment, the basis of long-term decision-making is seriously flawed. Children may be re-abused, or kept in permanent care unnecessarily (Shearer 1989)[5].

Resources

It is evident that effective child protection investigation work requires the provision of resources — for the training and supervision of social workers and their managers, as well as the time and space to do the work and recover from its demands.

Other resource issues which spring to mind are the need to ensure safety for the worker, which can mean using two workers to investigate. I discuss safety in more detail below.

Another important, but often ignored, resource issue is that of administrative support. The quality of administrative systems, and the accuracy with which information is retrieved, have a crucial effect on the quality of the investigation and the protection of the child. The provision of adequate typing support is also fundamental, reflecting the importance of accurate, detailed, and contemporaneous recording of investigations. These are vital to the success of subsequent court proceedings to protect the child.

Supervision

However, the existence of clear procedures and principles and of adequate resources is not enough to ensure good practice; it is necessary to look to the effect families have on the workers who investigate. Unless these effects are recognised and acknowledged, our investigations will not be effective in protecting abused children (cf Morrison T. 1990)[6]. Workers in this field must receive regular supervision which includes close supervision throughout the investigation. This means that managers need to be available out of hours to provide this service to workers. Effective supervision of child protection investigation can only be provided by supervisors who are themselves receiving supervision. Otherwise, the supervisor is vulnerable to meeting his legitimate professional needs inappropriately through the supervisory relationship and thus restricting his freedom and power to challenge collusion (cf Morrison T. 1989).[7]

It is essential that supervision focuses on the worker's feelings about his work. Unless his feelings of anger, sadness, guilt and helplessness are confronted and validated in supervision, they are likely to obstruct the worker's ability to focus on the child during an investigation, and engender either collusion to deny abuse at one end of the spectrum or persecution of parents at the other.

Supervision is also necessary to enable workers to develop clarity about minimum acceptable standards of child care. Without this opportunity workers will be vulnerable to collusion when they investigate, either because they become used to poor standards and their perceptions become distorted — 'all families on benefit have to live like this' — or because they suffer what Olive Stevenson (1989)[8] calls 'white, liberal immobilisation', e.g. 'Black families have stricter discipline than we do.'

The principle that child protection workers need supervision holds good no matter how experienced the workers; we need to recognise, without criticism, that the pressure exerted on us by parents to collude, deny or minimise, is very powerful and increases according to the seriousness of the abuse. Good supervision constitutes one element of protection for the worker. It can also ensure that the voice of the child is heard.

The investigation — keeping the child in focus
Initial referral

The quality of the initial referral is the bedrock of the subsequent investigation and decision-making process. Taking a detailed referral requires time and skill and is the first opportunity to focus on the child.

It is essential that *all* referrals are taken seriously, irrespective of the source of the referral. Some workers assume that anonymous, or drunken referrals, or those from separated parents seeking custody, will be malicious. This is a comforting assumption, but is regrettably, unfounded. The referrer's view about possible violent reprisals by the family should also be taken seriously as an indicator of possible risk to the investigating worker.

Information gathering

The investigation of abuse allegations must be set in the context of any previous knowledge about the family; otherwise a pattern of injuries or history of neglect may be missed and wrong decisions taken. Checking the Child Protection Register and consulting with line managers are the first steps; action and time-scale must be agreed at this point, and the child should certainly be seen within twenty-four hours.

Previous information about the family will be available from a number of sources, such as health visitors, schools, and nurseries. It is essential to ask specific questions about past and present concerns, and to bear in mind the possibility that professionals' opinion about the likelihood of abuse may be biased, for example, by the nature of their own relationship with the parents. If the parents have presented up to now as pleasant and co-operative, important signs from the child may easily be minimised or dismissed.

At this stage, it should *never* be concluded that the child is safe from abuse. This can only be done at the conclusion of the investigation after the child, siblings and parent(s) have been seen and interviewed. The views of professionals should be noted, but must not be allowed to obscure later evidence of abuse.

Where an investigation is required on a case already known to a social worker, the risk of pre-judgement and bias is high. The worker may feel her past decisions are undermined if abuse is found. She may have developed a relationship with the parent which obscures her role of authority in relation to child protection matters. ('This Mum really loves her children, and has a good relationship with me.') The need for close supervision is even greater here, and the use of clear contracts in long term work with clients is essential to help avoid such collusion.

The worker's right to safety should be considered, bearing in mind any information from the referrer, or from police records which indicates a history of violence. In the absence of such information or opinion, the worker's and/or manager's 'gut feelings' about possible danger should *not* be ignored. This attention to the safety of the worker is not only important in terms of the worker's rights, however. It also has crucial implications for the process of the investigation, because social workers cannot exercise their authority appropriately and investigate effectively if they feel unsafe or afraid. The risk that they will placate the parents out of fear, without even realising they have done so, must be recognised. Social workers and their managers should not hesitate to request police attendance at investigations whenever this is felt to be necessary. Such a police presence will be purely to allow the investigation to proceed in an orderly way and without threat or intimidation to the worker. It does not necessarily imply a joint investigation. I remember realising only as I drove home from an investigation how scared I had felt. I had been so busy with other tasks and issues, I had not allowed myself to feel the subtle but definite intimidation offered by this father.

It is important that workers are aware of their feelings, and can use them confidently as a further source of information about the environment which the parents provide for the child in his daily life.

Already, before we have reached the child's home to see him and his parents, a number of features and processes can be operating to distract the worker from her focus on the child. These processes may arise out of the worker's prejudice, work pressures, or difficult feelings.

'Anonymous referrals are usually malicious.' 'There's not time to do *another* investigation this week.' 'I don't want to go to this home — it might be violent.' 'I can't face taking little children away from their parents.'

The supervisor's task is to enable the worker to cut through her rationalisations and establish openly the worker's resistance. Once recognised, such resistance is more easily left behind so that the investigation can proceed with the child as its central focus. The worker's 'antennae' can be tuned in more accurately to the child.

Seeing the family

This is the most important phase of information-gathering; it is also the most difficult in terms of remaining focused on the child. The worker is now on the parents' territory and needs to recognise this by treating them with respect whilst insisting on the need to investigate. Most parents want to be investigated 'without being investigated': — 'It would be all right if it was true, if someone had reported something that was right' (Morrison T., Guilfoyle P. and Masson H., 1990).[9]

Resistance

It is important then that investigating social workers realise that the investigation, no matter how professionally performed, *will* be traumatic for parents. It is not surprising then that either overtly or covertly they will attempt to keep control of the process in various ways. In order to investigate effectively social workers need to respond sensitively but authoritatively to parents: often a difficult balance to achieve. Social workers need training and supervision in order to deal effectively with parents' resistance to being investigated; otherwise this resistance will prevent the worker from establishing that the child's needs are being met (cf. Dale *et al.*, 1986).[10] Individual workers are vulnerable to different kinds of resistance and emotional pressure from parents, and need to use supervision to become aware of these. Some parents present as timid victims who subtly convey the message that the worker must look after *them* and see to their needs (*passive-helpless*). It is vital that the worker recognises that the parent is putting himself *before* the children, and that this is indicative of unmet needs which prevent the child's needs being appropriately met.

Others try to drive workers away without investigating an allegation by arguing every point at length or wanting to discuss who referred the case. It is important to recognise this as a distraction from the main task and an attempt to keep control of the investigation. Other parents may attempt to use aggressive 'tantrums' as a way of shifting the focus from the children and the investigation and of intimidating the worker into leaving without completing her task (*challenging/chaotic*).

'*Hostile*' resistance is overt, highly threatening and may involve the use of physical force on members of staff. Its impact is frightening and immobilising, and its use can mean that workers become 'psychological hostages' to the parents; where this is unacknowledged by the investigator, the danger to the child is high. It is essential that instead of 'coping' and accommodating to hostility, workers acknowledge their fears and get help to complete their task. The case of Kimberlay Carlile is a tragic example of this process (Blom-Cooper 1987).[11]

Passive aggression is a particularly difficult form of resistance to deal with as parents are superficially co-operative, but this presentation masks a hidden reservoir of explosive anger which can be fatal, as in the case of Jasmine Beckford, where parents appeared co-operative. In fact, they were covertly 'in charge' of the professional's plans (Blom-Cooper 1985).[12]

It is also essential that workers are constantly aware that parents can and do lie very plausibly, whatever method they use to resist.

Most parents, however, are generally co-operative, and therefore it is useful to view a substantial level of resistance, distraction and intimidation presented to the worker as significant information which may indicate that all is not well for the child. Certainly it gives useful information about the parents' ways of dealing with difficult situations in general. It is useful to note the child's responses to a parent in this instance. They may freeze, or seem unaffected by the loudest of tirades, or go to comfort their parent. All of these show how the child has adapted to parental behaviour over time.

Parents who show no emotion at all during the investigation and accept it passively and without interest are of concern in terms of their ability to meet their children's emotional needs.

My argument here is not, then, that parents should not have feelings about being investigated: feelings of anger, fear, guilt and shame are natural and understandable. The key issue is whether the parents can, with the workers' help, set these feelings aside sufficiently to allow the investigation to proceed in a calm and orderly way which disrupts the children as little as possible. In other words, workers should expect parents to be capable of putting the needs of their child before their own strong feelings during the investigation.

The contract

Investigation at the child's home can be enormously facilitated by using some relatively simple techniques to deal with the parents' feelings and create a structure for the ensuing investigation (cf. Erooga and Masson 1990).[13] It is essential to be open and honest at the outset about the reason for the visit. This, of course, is impossible unless the worker feels safe. Research on parents' experience of investigation indicates that they appreciate such honesty and clarity (Morrison T., Guilfoyle P. and Masson H., unpublished research, 1990).

Initially, a general statement such as 'I am X, from Y agency, and I need to see you about a call we have received about your family. Can I come in to discuss it?' is a helpful way into the home. Parents need to be asked to wait to hear the details of the allegation until the worker has explained what will happen during the investigation. This is the start of making a contract with the parents about how they will behave during the investigation.

It is particularly important to ask parents how they would show the worker if they got angry and what they would do. The worker needs to feel sure that the parents will not be violent and the ideal contract is for the parent to agree to *tell* the worker when he is feeling angry. This part of the contract is most important in establishing the worker's control over the situation and thus reducing her own anxieties about violence, as well as setting clear expectations of the parents' behaviour in order to reduce any distress to the child.

The next stage is to explain that the parents will be told the allegation(s), and given the opportunity to respond; that the worker will need to see all the children and their rooms, as well as kitchen cupboards, and fridge etc., where allegations of neglect are concerned. Parents need to be asked specifically to co-operate and give their consent. They should be told that the worker will give honest feedback after these tasks are done. The worker may also want to let parents know that she will review her observations away from the family before giving feedback; 'taking a break' can be very helpful in ensuring the focus has remained on the child.

This second stage of the contract is helpful in enabling parents to co-operate by giving them information about what they can expect during the investigation and can go some way to reducing their natural anxieties about the process.

Parents' feelings

It is also necessary to directly address the parents' feelings during the investigation. This involves commenting on any observable emotion (or indeed lack of emotion) and asking what it is about. Often just the chance to say he is angry that he has been 'reported' allows a parent to set his anger aside and hear what he is being told. Anger may give way to tears or trembling and often masks fear that children will be removed. False reassurance should never be offered; workers need to assure parents they will be honest even about the most difficult subjects and to emphathise with these understandable feelings. The *only* honest answer about removal at this point is 'I don't know.'

It is important to take time to listen to the parents and be clear about what they are feeling and why. This not only allows the parent to set aside strong feelings which prevent him hearing what is being said, and engaging in co-operating with the investigation; it can also provide useful information about the parent's attitude to and relationship with the child.

This process of dealing with parents' feelings often needs to be done a number of times during the visit: indeed, as often as the worker becomes aware that the parent's feelings are overwhelming him, i.e. when it is clear he cannot listen. Workers need to be aware too that feelings may be 'put on' for the worker's benefit, and to rely on their own responses in assessing the genuineness of the parents' expressed feelings. Asking about the parent's feelings can also be most helpful in stopping fruitless 'content' debates or 'tantrums', though it is also important to recognise that some parents need quite clear instructions in these circumstances, e.g. 'I want you to stop shouting and stay in the room while I explain what will happen next.'

7 Child abuse investigation

Seeing the child

The child needs to be seen to establish if there are any injuries or suspicious marks. Unless the child *is* marked, even if the worker believes the child has been hit, there can be no basis for future investigation in physical abuse cases, though, of course, help can still be offered and concerns expressed and fully recorded for future reference, particularly where parents deny hitting the child.

Undressing the child should be done with the parents' consent, in their presence, and preferably by them. Teenagers may need to be checked by a health visitor or GP, for example when a girl is being investigated by a male worker. The inspection of the child's body by the social worker is *not* a medical examination. Although a skin check is necessary to rule out nappy rash and bruising for instance, so the child's private parts must be *seen*, there are *no circumstances in which the child's genitals or anus should be examined more closely* by the social worker.

Parents should be asked several times in the course of the investigation how any marks occurred, and a demonstration of the incident is useful. Changes in explanation or lack of explanation are significant.

The child should be also seen away from the parent, with the parent's consent which will usually already have been given at the initial contracting stage. It is important to engage the child in an age-appropriate way and to explain who you are and why you have come, and to offer general reassurance. 'It is my job to make sure children are safe and happy.' The child should be told of the allegations, and asked for a response, and if marks have been seen, his explanation should be sought. Clearly many abused children will be unable to be open with the worker for fear of reprisals from parents, or because they genuinely see the abuse as their fault. It is, therefore, essential to assess not only what the child says, but his demeanour, his emotional state, and his relationship with his parent(s). Abused and neglected children may appear affectionate and unafraid of a parent. Many have become well-adapted to placating and/or parenting their own parents, and so the parents' efforts to reach out to the child are a more certain indication of a healthy bond than the child's approaches to the parent. Clearly then it is also essential to observe child and parent together, as well, during the investigation.

Siblings

It is important to see and talk to the referred child's siblings, and to treat seriously what they say. They may have witnessed abuse and/or may themselves have been abused. Whilst investigating allegations of facial bruising to two siblings, I undressed a third, younger, child to find purple bruising in the shape of a bite-mark to his buttuck. Listening to all the children in the household is important.

Other essential information

The investigation should ensure that a family history is obtained, including factual details, any history of parents' own childhood abuse, and that parents are given the opportunity to discuss problems they may experience with the child. When parents admit they have injured the children, the worker needs to be sure that they understand how this occurred, that the parent accepts full responsibility for the injury, shows an appropriate emotional response (e.g. concern for the child, remorse) and demonstrates an ability to avoid hitting the child again. The role of the non-abusing parent also needs to be understood; no investigation is complete until *all* adults in the house have been interviewed. It will, on occasion, be appropriate to check their details with the police.

Review of information and feedback to parents

It can be very useful for the investigator to use another room or her car to review the investigation away from the family when the initial enquiries are complete.

Such a break allows joint invetigators to share and check out perceptions and the feelings the family evokes in them. Feelings in the professional can often mirror feelings which are occurring in the family. If the investigator is alone, this distancing from the family can allow the gaps in information, the inconsistencies or changes of explanation and the questions that are too frightening to ask parents to come to the surface and be acknowledged. At this point the gaps in information may be significant, and indicative, for instance, that an apparently co-operative parent is not being open. This break allows the worker to decide what needs to happen next in order to complete the investigation. This may be a medical examination, or feedback to the parents about any concerns which do not require medical examination (e.g. wet mattresses, standards of hygiene, etc.) It may also include a decision to refer on to the police for criminal investigation in serious cases.

Medical examinations

Any marks to the child which the worker decides are suspicious should be medically examined, *regardless of the apparent need for*

7 Child abuse investigation

treatment. Workers who are not medically trained are not qualified to make medical judgements. The medical examination confirms the existence of injuries, which may be necessary for court proceedings. It will also establish whether other, possibly internal, injuries exist.

It is important that the social worker attends the medical examination to inform the doctor of explanations offered and the basis for suspicion and concern. On occasions it is possible for doctors to give a clear diagnosis of abuse based on the injuries and explanations given. Often this is not possible, however, and the need to take the child's statements seriously in decision making is once again essential, though easily forgotten.

Decision-making

It is essential to consult with the line manager *before* taking a decision about the level of protection required by the child. The manager's task is to ensure the procedures have been followed, and to deal with any feeling of 'stuckness' which the worker may experience. Sometimes workers may reflect the parents' perspective of denial or minimisation, whilst at other times, they may feel powerless and immobilised, mirroring the child's position. The manager's responsibility is to ensure that the investigative tasks are completed and that the basis for protection decisions are clear to himself and the worker. The manager needs a clear contract with the worker to give permission to explore and validate feelings, as well as to challenge the worker's views. Without such supervision, the worker and manager may fail to protect the child appropriately because the power of the parents in covertly influencing workers to collude with them remains unacknowledged and unchallenged.

The following issues must be considered in deciding the need for immediate protection. Please note that the decision-making criteria for sexual abuse are different. In particular, it is *never* safe for victim and perpetrator to remain together, and obviously, it is preferable that the perpetrator leaves the home.

1. The nature and severity of the injury/neglect, combined with the age of the child.
2. Any history of previous abuse or neglect, of previous care episodes, or concerns about poor parenting.
3. Any history of the parents being victims of abuse as children.
4. The degree of denial/minimisation by the parent.
5. The attitude of the non-abusing parent, and the degree to which (s)he acknowledges responsibility for failure to protect.

6. The parents' willingness to recognise problems and any past indicators of ability to use help.
7. The extent to which the parents can be trusted to co-operate with the authorities in future.
8. The parent's ability to control his anger: how realistic are any guarantees that it won't happen again. Failure to give such a guarantee is significant.
9. The parents' attitude to the child, including the degree to which the investigation itself places the child at risk. Again, guarantees must be specifically sought.
10. The child's wishes. Contrary to popular opinion, few children, even if abused, want to be away from home. Such a wish should, therefore, be taken seriously and fully explored, if necessary over a period of time.

Concluding the investigation

Parents also need to know the outcome of the investigation whether concerns exist or not. 'Where allegations or suspicions prove unfounded, this should be made explicitly clear to parents' (*Working Together*, DHSS 1988)[14]. They should be kept informed at all stages. The conclusion of the investigation where abuse is suspected or known is the Child Protection Case Conference. Workers should inform parents of the views they will take to that conference and obtain, possibly in writing, the views of the parents.

Conclusion

Social workers who investigate abuse allegations must be trained and subsequently supervised in a way which enables them to recognise the subtle and covert influences which abusing parents can bring to bear to prevent them from detecting abuse and acting to protect children. Otherwise sound principles, clear procedures, adequate resources and good intentions will still fail children who may then pass on the painful inheritance of abuse to the next generation:

> The normal reactions to injury should be anger and pain; since children in this hurtful kind of environment, however, are forbidden to express their anger, and since it would be unbearable to experience their pain all along, they are compelled to suppress their feelings, repress all memory of trauma, and idealise those guilty of the abuse. Later they will have no memory of what was done to them (Alice Miller, 1983).[15]

7 Child abuse investigation

References

1. Erooga, M. and Masson, H. (1990) *Journeys into the Unknown*, Rochdale Child Abuse Training Sub-Committee.
2. Miller, Alice (1983) *For Your Own Good*, Faber & Faber.
3. Blom-Cooper, L. (1987) *A Child in Mind*, Greenwich Borough Council.
4. Dingwall, R., *et al.* (1983) *The Protection of Children*, Blackwell.
5. Shearer, E. (1989) 'Child Sexual Abuse: Issues for Treatment Work with Families', in *Context*, No. 4 (Winter 1989), Association for Family Therapy.
6. Morrison, T. (1990) 'The Emotional Effects of Child Protection Work on the Worker,' speech to BASPCAN Spring Conference, April 1990. Unpublished.
7. Morrison, T. (1989) 'Safe for Action,' in *Community Care*, 26.10.89.
8. Stevenson, O. (1989) 'What Does Training Have To Offer To Inter-professional Work?' Occasional Paper No. 7. NSPCC.
9. Morrison, T., Guilfoyle, P. and Masson H. (1990), unpublished research on 'Parents' Perceptions of the Investigation Process.'
10. Dale, P. *et al* (1986) *Dangerous Families*, Tavistock.
11. Blom-Cooper, L. (1987), op. cit.
12. Blom-Cooper, L. (1985) *A Child In Trust*, Brent Borough Council.
13. Erooga, M. and Masson, H. (1990) op. cit.
14. *Working Together* (1988) DHSS.
15. Miller, A. (1990). *The Untouched Key: Tracing Childhood. Trauma in Creativity and Destructiveness.* Virago.

8 Learning to listen to children

Euan M. Ross

Introduction

Communicating with children is a different matter from being kind to or fond of them, or being very skilled at coping with their daily needs. Writing as a children's doctor one recalls that, whilst there are times when technical excellence is the greatest need, there are occasions, particularly in children's surgery, where lack of communication skills and inability to listen to children leads to misdiagnosis. The equivalent occurs in other professions who work for and with children. Time and again one reads of the childhood unhappinesses expressed in the autobiographies of the famous — how much more common this must be in the unpublished annals of the poor. I think I became a paediatrician because of experiences at the age of seven whilst having my tonsils removed. Having empathy and thus the ability to communicate with children is a skill which can be learned. Is it laziness or some inherent defect of character if one persists in a career involving children without becoming aware of one's lack of listening skills and seeking to improve them?

One can only fully learn about a child's needs from first-hand knowledge. Despite the well-established transatlantic practice of telephone consultations there is no real substitute for direct observation. One cannot communicate with a sleeping child. This was well demonstrated by the death of Jasmine Beckford from abuse — the children had been observed at sleep in a darkened room, their social worker had been assured that they were well and did not wish to disturb them, thus Jasmine was not examined in her final months.

8 Learning to listen to children

The moral is that if you do not wish to disturb you must make a point of returning until you are satisfied that you have seen the child in an active state, functioning normally.

Whilst this chapter was written with child abuse in mind it is meant to apply to all occasions when people in a professional capacity interact with children. Hopefully much will be seen to be commonsense and apply to everyday parenting. Do 'professional people' — to give a generic title that in this chapter covers a host of social workers, doctors, nurses, therapists, teachers, police, magistrates and various 'ologists' (putting them in no rank order of significance) — have any inbuilt or preordained particular ability to communicate with children? I think not. It is only in recent years that the insights of those who have made deep study into the needs of children have trickled into everyday practice. Still one finds a minority of those in responsible posts in connection with children who have little ability to relate to them.

In the UK there has been a welcome improvement in communication with children thanks to organisations such as the National Association for Welfare of Children in Hospital (NAWCH) and NSPCC in the social work field but there remains plenty of room for improvement. In many countries needless rules and restrictions are still imposed; where you see white coats or stern notices about visiting hours, suspect other less visible barriers to true communication between professionals, parents and children. For all her faults and understanding I think there has been more progress in child-centred professional work in the UK than in some other countries that I have visited.

Staff selection and training

Twenty years ago the concept of child abuse had hardly been recognised, and naturally did not figure in professional training let alone formal teaching in communication skills. It thus can be expected that professional workers aged much over 40 will have had little systematic training in their undergraduate courses on matters specific to child abuse and will have had to rely on whatever postgraduate training they have attended. It can be assumed that in many instances this will have been fragmented and unplanned.

How do we train ourselves, our students and our seniors to listen to children? The right attitudes are needed at the top in any training organisation. Senior members need to teach by example (as well as in the classroom) the concepts of self-knowledge about personal strengths and weaknesses. There are times when they have to take the difficult step of asking the very questions that those more junior to themselves would like to ask but do not dare. They must be seen going to the more elementary low-level training sessions. If they are too proud to go as delegates, they should get themselves invited as speakers and stay for the whole course leaving others to go to the 'cannot be missed' committees that steal their days.

Visual aids and hindrances

Students are often hidden behind one-way screens to observe developmental assessments and psychiatric interviews. It is important that teachers are properly trained in their use. It is all too easy to forget the student. Screens should be used very sparingly. There are quite enough children with problems for one or two students to join sessions. Often they can be a useful intermediary. Well-made video films in small doses are good for demonstrating teaching points; they must be made to full professional standards and very heavily edited if they are not to be far too long and teach incorrect lessons. Videos must be watched with a teacher present who can stop the tape when appropriate and start immediate discussion. Otherwise they can readily become a bore.

How do we listen to children?

Total listening uses all one's senses and includes seeing, smelling, feeling as well as hearing. Usually it is a joy to listen to children but not always. It can be exhausting. What one is told may worry one greatly; often a great deal of time is needed before a child can unburden their mind to you. A hint that you are not really interested or need to be doing something else will destroy the relationship.

Much of one's experience with adults is highly relevant to children — remember the times when you have been angry with professional people, even felt like going to law? Your problem probably had its basis in 'Nobody listened to me' rather than incompetence in knowledge or action — 'I could have told him that.'

Those who speak do not always say what they mean — listeners must be able to hear between the lines, in a medical context. A request — 'Can I have some more of the cough mixture?' — may be followed by a lingering grasp on the door handle — 'While I'm here, doctor...' Then the real problem pours out — the pornographic magazines that her husband brings home, the worries about the child's oversexualised language. One is told these tales only if one is ready to hear them. The perils to the child if one is not prepared to listen can be very serious. 'I did not tell the doctor as he is always so busy.' Other professions can quote parallel scenarios.

All that applies to adults applies to children but there is more:

8 Learning to listen to children

The setting — permission to speak

The surroundings must be right. They must be child-friendly with appearance appropriate to children, though one must cater for a wide range of ages and tastes. Let your clinic/office look like a happy child's own room. The listening person must seem right, look right, smell right, and arrange their setting appropriately.

Very minor and inexpensive measures can make a great difference in the appearance of a room. If forensic interviews are to be undertaken, video cameras may be needed. They and their microphones need to be as unthreatening as possible.

The listener must look credible to the child and those who bring the child along. Neither the starched collar nor the torn jeans! All too often professional workers overwhelm children. In an attempt to ingratiate the child they ask their name or age, forgetting that young children are unused to meeting someone who does not know them already. Even worse is to get the child's name wrong. Many children are known by quite different names from the one written on their records. Most of all get the gender right. Children hate being accused of being the wrong age or gender! A few enquiries behind the scenes can get the relationship right from the start.

How much privacy is needed? Is a chaperon needed? How many should be in the room? Not a herd of students. Remember that people will talk about most intimate matters to empathic strangers, e.g. radio phone-ins.

Ways of listening

Children need time to sum up new situations; semi-ignore them, set out your room with appropriate books, crayons, paper. Do not provide toys/playthings for the wrong age, wrong sex and sometimes race. If you get it wrong the child may rightly regard you as a fool who is not to be trusted.

One of the great differences in child and adult behaviour is the desire to draw. Few adults draw, children do it every day. Even if your attempts at verbal communication are failing, paper and pencil offer the best alternative. If you speak different languages you can still communicate through drawings. Sometimes children will only express their emotions through a drawing. Do not ask children to draw something complicated. Ask them to draw a picture of where they live and see what happens. When looking at the drawing do not over-interpret it; has a happy or a sad picture been drawn? What size are the family members? Is one member much larger than others? What are they doing? Have genitalia been drawn? Recently I saw a six year old boy brought because of 'behaviour problems'. He told me that he would draw a picture of the ghost that lived in his house. Mysteriously he told me that the ghost had no kidneys. The ghost turned out to be an elder sibling born anephric who died when 24 hours old. This child was the replacement.

Examinations can be sped up if parents are routinely asked to bring up some recent school books.

Who should do the listening:

Those with ears to hear. Those who cannot listen to adults can be assumed to be incapable of listening to children.

Some people of high academic ability are very poor listeners — they may be 'too full of themselves' and whilst they have achieved high positions may be unsuitable for this aspect of their work and thus not interested in teaching the subject. The recent emergence of community paediatrics as a medical subspeciality should lead to a cadre of doctors who have a special interest and capabilities in the subject.

What we must not do is to subject people — children or adults — to repeated cross-examination. Detective work is for trained detectives, not the rest of us. Stories change, either time heals or magnifies, often a bit of both so that the truth may remain hazy.

Special attention needs to be paid to:

The pregnant mother who appears to be hostile to her pregnancy or new baby, the mother who has made no physical preparation for her new baby. In the early days of life one can identify at least five different types of cry — pain, hunger, boredom, illness and the cerebral cry of the brain injured baby. Watch the child feeding and smiling and the baby's expressions of both contentment and anger. Learn to recognise the older abused child who develops frozen watchfulness, who cringes readily, as well as the one who 'settles in easily' — who is over-friendly to any stranger who shows the slightest interest.

Children speak with meaning at very varying ages. All parents know to be careful what they say in front of children — and know the embarrassments that can occur. Students need to learn a great deal about normal and abnormal child development. It is essential that they appreciate how great are the variations among normal children. This particularly applies to the rate of development of speech. Some have a much earlier ability not only to speak but to communicate effectively. At last legal authorities are appreciating this fact. In general children speak the truth as they understand it. Peter Ustinov recalled how following Sunday School teaching he refused to visit Father Christmas at Harrods in London, mistaking it for an establishment run by King Herod.

Is the child telling the truth?

It is too easy to be wrong — all of us tend to say the thing that we feel is wanted of us. We all know that children's understanding of truth is a developing matter. Children are blessed with insight and imagination that tends to be lost or knocked out of us as we age. Children may be very protective towards an abusive parent and may have been threatened with dire consequences if they tell the truth — remember Oliver Twist.

Many countries are now setting up forms of telephone Helplines, and we have a great deal to learn about their role and use and abuse. Fortunately the organisations that run them are putting great effort into training their telephone listeners.

Can't speak the language?

One can over-readily assume that immigrant people in the UK do not know any English. Interpreters cannot be guaranteed to give a true translation and may give a 'sanitised' version. Do not fall into the trap of believing that only people of the same race and culture understand each other. Beware caste differences or intraracial disputes or collusion. Some men find the concept of senior professional women workers, especially social workers, very difficult to relate to.

One trap is to be deceived because a patient/client happens to be part of the extended family or a private patient of a colleague. Another problem is the very high social class or famous parent who has the skills to manipulate their child's professional helpers. I recall great problems where the father was a barrister, the mother a solicitor, and their child was showing signs of abuse. A member of one's golf club or church, as well as the rich and famous, can all be associated with child abuse. It is vital that if personal loyalties are involved, one steps aside and makes sure that a totally non-involved colleague takes over.

Within a country, be it the UK, France, or even a small country such as Holland, the child's dialect and yours may be quite different. Words describing child behaviour let alone their genitalia can be totally different even within a country. How many words for penis can be recorded in the UK? How many English know that the Scots expression for unemployment benefit is 'on the buroo' (pronounced brew) or the subtle difference between 'girning' and 'greetin'[7]? Some words may be so naughty in the family context that they cannot be spoken. Few non-medical people whatever their age and education know where their major internal organs are or what they do. It has been estimated that doctors learn 10,000 new words during their training. They emerge with very different concepts – say of the stomach or the bowels – from that of society as a whole and forget that they can easily be talking at cross purposes even with other professionals such as lawyers.

Time

It takes time to make a trusting relationship with a child and family. Whilst most professional people are genuinely and sometimes grossly overworked and have to limit the time they spend on any one case, it can be too easy to plead lack of time in taking short cuts. Sometimes the answer may lie in better management of the limited time that one has. Advice and training in managing one's time may be needed. Time is easily dissipated in writing over-long reports or attending too many meetings. Some, without realising it, actually enjoy the role of worker-martyr. Some have treatable health problems that limit efficiency. It is all too easy to become insidiously unfit and marginally yet chronically depressed and become over-cautious and thus unable to sort the wood from the trees. Some with these problems were badly taught or are poorly supervised. Listening, whether as part of one's professional work, or for pleasure, has to be taught. Listeners' courses in music are held but I have never heard of one that concentrates on teaching professional listening.

Interviewing the child

The first and cardinal principle in medical education is not physical examination but history taking. This in itself can be powerfully therapeutic and is one of the core skills of a doctor — but is not mastered by all. Similar history taking skills are needed by all in the caring professions. There are certain aspects to this craft which are often overlooked:

Ask structured questions in a set order so that one does not leave out relevant areas.
Make accurate and legible records: always writing down in precis where necessary the gist of what the patient actually said: if they say 'I have pain in the arse', do not write 'proctalgia'. If the patient

8 Learning to listen to children

actually says 'proctalgia' they may have looked up the word in a book but there is no guarantee that this actually is the correct diagnosis! **Beware the leading question.** all too often the amateur asks a question that suggests only one answer: a child has a large mark probably caused by a whip over the back — 'what did daddy hit you with?' That is a typical leading question. Try again: 'I see you have a red mark on your back. Can you tell me how it happened?' Record the answers you get. If you ask leading questions you are very likely to get the answer that the interviewee thinks you want!

The standard way that medical students are taught to take history starts with: 'Why have you come to see me?' — then the **History of the main presenting problem** followed by the: **Previous (medical) history** then the:

Family history

Including the health of mother, father, siblings. It is important that you as well as the patient decide what is relevant and that deaths in the family are disclosed.

Social history

The housing, where the family live, their moves, how far from relatives, who is in work and what do they do, are there major social problems? Transport, amenities, even sometimes the name of the dog! There is a fine line between being gratuitously nosy and getting vital and relevant information.

Childbirth and development

Health in pregnancy, where born, birth weight, details of delivery, health as a new baby, feeding patterns. The ages at which the child did things such as walking, talking, nursery and school experience and grades.

Then you can start to examine. With any luck the child will be playing or drawing. Note if they separate from parent or not, whether their behaviour is age-appropriate. Do child and parent interact, talk to each other, reassure each other, cling or seem indifferent? Does the parent speak ill of the child in their hearing? Does the child speak ill of the parent?

Physical examination

The medical profession is expected to examine and thus see their patients undressed. Even the process of undressing can yield valuable information. The outer and especially underclothes make important statements. Are they appropriate, too many or too few? Their cost, condition and appropriateness tells a great deal about parental values; are they and the child clean? Obsession about cleanliness too is an important sign.

It has now become exceptional for a child to be smelly or dressed in worn clothes — does the child over-readily part with clothes, or refuse? Some children are most hesitant to let their genital regions be inspected, others immediately masturbate. Watch for spontaneous over-sexualised speech. I find the time well spent watching this process out of the corner of my eye and do not want pre-stripped children brought to me. This often tells me more than actual physical inspection of the genitalia and anus where, unless there has been very recent trauma or repeated buggery, there are generally no convincing physical signs to confirm or deny that penetrative sexual abuse has occurred.

In the course of any examination it may dawn on you that the child may have been sexually abused. You are now confronted with an ethical dilemma. You know that repeated physical examination is contraindicated; if you have not had forensic training your findings are likely to be wide open to challenge. You also know that only a fresh collection of secretions for bacteriology and detection of spermatazoa will be of any forensic value and that ano-genital tears heal rapidly. You may know something of disclosure techniques and that a set of anatomically correct dolls is to hand. You are in a highly fraught area. Unless you are appropriately trained the correct course is to complete your examination in the conventional way inspecting the ano-genital regions as you would in any other paediatric examination, making careful records of what you see at the same time. You should remember to look at the skin, fundi, eardrums and upper lip fraenum, making careful, dated and signed notes as you go. You should ensure an immediate forensic examination by those appointed to undertake one in line with the Child Protection procedures for your area. The use of anatomically correct dolls should be left to those trained in this field. Although many such dolls have been bought in recent years there is much difference of opinion concerning their validity: just because a child finds them interesting and may try some suggestive experiments with them does not prove that they have been abused or are grossly precocious.

'I took her to the doctor about the cough but she did not give me anything for it and all at once she was showing her some disgusting dolls. I would not stand for it and am not going back to that doctor. Filthy mind she has.'

8 Learning to listen to children

Staff training

As a manager, particularly a recently appointed one, you will have inherited most of your staff and it is usually a long time before you will have recruited your 'own' team. It is necessary to learn about their listening to children skills, yet you may find it difficult to get a chance to see them in action under real life situations. Role playing schemes can be a very good substitute. When interviewing your staff, make a list of the training in the subject that they have actually had. In a successful commercial business it is a general rule that about 5% of professional staff time needs to be spent on in-service training. The same is true for work with children. Remember that some become *less* skilled with the passage of time, and none can be expert in every aspect of their work.

Some are likely to have had much more recent training than others. Wherever possible exploit in-house skills for training. In-house teaching is far more cost-effective than sending people away on courses because the skills gained are shared in the department. When people do go on courses at the expense of your budget, insist that they write up notes and then give a presentation to the department so that everyone gains.

Identify those in the department who are poor listeners and communicators and institute remedial help. If they cannot make use of help, shoo them sideways and away from needy children.

Conclusion

Listening to children is not a vague concept or something that is purely a natural gift or even readily picked up. Listening and understanding what you hear requires a trained and practised ear. The quality of listening among those who work for children is greatly influenced by those who lead departments. If leaders have these skills, appreciate how they gained them, and are prepared to value and teach them to their colleagues, children will be better protected and their families will gain a great deal.

9 Persuading the courts to listen to children

J. R. Spencer

It is obviously important that the courts should be able to listen to children. Where criminal proceedings are taken against someone for an offence against a child, usually only two people know precisely what happened, one of whom is the child. For the criminal court to do justice in the case it is essential that it should listen to the child as well as to the defendant. As far as civil proceedings are concerned, Section 1 of the Children Act 1989 explicitly requires the court to have regard to 'the ascertainable wishes and feelings of the child concerned (considered in the light of his age and understanding)' when it is making decisions about a range of matters. The court cannot have regard to the child's wishes and feelings unless it can discover them, and to discover them it needs to listen to the child.

Yet important as it is that courts should be able to listen to children, the law has traditionally made it hard for them to do so. In the last two years there have been some important changes: but there is still a long way to go.

Discovering the child's wishes in civil proceedings

Here there are two methods by which the court can listen to the child.

Usually the court will receive information about the child's wishes indirectly as part of an official report. Depending on the type of proceedings, the reporter will be a probation officer working as a court welfare officer, a social worker, a guardian *ad litem* from the local panel, or a person from the Official Solicitor's department. This person will interview all those concerned, the child included, and transmit their news and views to the court in his report.

In principle, when an adult reports to the court what a child has told him this is hearsay, and hearsay is generally inadmissible as evidence (see below). If the hearsay rule applied without qualification to accounts of interviews contained in official reports this would obviously be most inconvenient, and the combined effect of several statutes and court decisions is to override the hearsay rule in connection with most statements contained in most official reports in most civil proceedings concerned with children. Some niggling doubts remain, however. Happily, these will be set to rest when the Children Act 1989 comes into force. Section 7 codifies the powers of the court to ask for reports from probation officers and social workers, and section 7(4) provides that

> Regardless of any enactment or rule of law which would otherwise prevent it from doing so, the court may take account of —
>
> (a) any statement contained in the report; and
>
> (b) any evidence given in respect of the matters referred to in the report,
>
> in so far as the statement or evidence is, in the opinion of the court, relevant to the question which it is considering.

Section 41(11) of the Act does the same for reports by guardians *ad litem*.

Alternatively, or in addition, the court may wish to hear the child's views from the child in person. When a court wants a person to communicate information for the purpose of deciding a disputed case it normally expects this to be done by means of oral evidence given on oath in open court. However, if the legal system wants a child to say truthfully which of two warring parents he or she would prefer to live with, putting the question in the presence of both parents and their lawyers is the most inept method that could be devised. Hence the superior courts have sanctioned a departure from traditional methods, and permit judges in custody disputes to interview children informally and in private. For wardships the practice was officially approved by the House of Lords in *Re K (Infants)* [1965] AC 201 many years ago, and the Court of Appeal has since approved it for proceedings other than wardships on a number of occasions. However, a tiresome problem arises where custody disputes are handled in the magistrates' courts, as they quite often are, because although the superior judges have officially approved of judges interviewing children in private, they have forbidden magistrates to do the same (*Re T* 4 Fam Law 48). Thus if a bench of magistrates wish to ascertain the child's views directly, they can only do so by getting him or her to give evidence in court — which means that in practice, if not in strict theory, they are often unable to listen to the child at all. If judges find it necessary to see children privately in order to do justice in custody disputes, there seems no intelligible reason why the magistrates should be forbidden to do the same.

Obtaining evidence from children about disputed matters of fact

The problems caused by *Re T* are nothing compared with the difficulties that the law puts in the way of the courts listening to children on disputed issues of fact — particularly where the disputed issue is whether an adult hurt or sexually abused them. Here, until recently, there was no question of the normal rules of evidence being waived. Indeed, where child witnesses are concerned the rules of evidence even contain several extra barriers erected with a view to making communication harder. In the case of children, there are three rules which operate together in such a way as to make it frequently impossible for the courts to listen to children. These are (i) the competency requirement, (ii) the requirement that evidence be given in open court, and (iii) the rule against hearsay evidence.

Competency

In principle, witnesses in England are expected to give sworn evidence, and are not competent to testify unless they 'understand the nature of an oath'. In the case of *Brasier* (1779) East PC 443, 1 Leach 199, the courts held that the rule that all evidence must be given on oath applies to little children as much as to adults. Indeed, the result of that decision was that the competency requirement applies more strictly to children than to adults, because whereas any adult who is not mentally subnormal is assumed to understand the nature of an oath, a child must always be examined to discover whether this is so, and is not permitted to give evidence if he or she does not. When *Brasier* was decided, and for a century or so afterwards, 'understanding the nature of an oath' meant believing that you would go to Hell for ever if you lied. With growing public scepticism about eternal damnation, however, the judges turned 'the nature of an oath' into little more than a solemn promise to tell the truth with the name of God attached: a development recognised by Parliament when it changed the form of an oath a child must take

9 Persuading the courts to listen to children

from 'I swear before Almighty God' to 'I promise before Almighty God' in the Children and Young Persons' Act 1963. Then in *Hayes* (1977) 64 CrApR 194 the Court of Appeal watered it down still further, ruling that a child who had never heard of God, Jesus or the Bible was competent to take an oath if he or she

> ...has a sufficient appreciation of the solemnity of the occasion, and the added responsibility to tell the truth, which is involved in taking an oath, over and above the duty to tell the truth which is an ordinary duty of normal social conduct.

Surprisingly, however, this ruling is sometimes overlooked. In a much publicised case in Exeter in 1988 a judge refused to allow a girl aged ten to give sworn evidence because of her lack of religious knowledge — which, because of the corroboration requirement that then existed (see below), meant that the prosecution case collapsed.

In the days when 'understanding the nature of an oath' meant believing in Hell fire and damnation, the competency requirement was a very serious obstacle to the court's ability to listen to children. Rosa Waugh, the daughter of Benjamin Waugh who founded the NSPCC, gives the following example in her biography of her father.[1]

> The counsel defending objected to the child's evidence being taken, on the ground that she was 'too young to understand the nature of an oath'. Thereupon the judge asked her to come closer to him, which she did with great reluctance. She was put on to the table just underneath him. Then from above he said in his kindest voice, 'What do you know, my child, about the Supreme Being?' The child looked for a moment at the most terrible-looking man she had ever seen in her short life, hesitated, and then, perhaps naturally, began to cry. 'I do not think I can take this evidence,' said the judge. The counsel for the prosecution, anxious not to lose the evidence, obtained leave from the judge to try his hand — so, by way of making matters easier, said, also in his kindest voice, 'Now, my dear, who is God?' The child, being still unable to give any reply, satisfactory or otherwise, was put down.

Finding the competency requirement caused great difficulties in prosecuting people for cruelty to children. Along with other organisations, the NSPCC mounted a public campaign to get the law changed to allow young children to give unsworn evidence. After an uphill struggle they succeeded, and children were permitted to give unsworn evidence at trials for certain sexual offences by a provision of the Criminal Law Amendment Act of 1885. In later Acts of

Parliament this provision was gradually extended to prosecutions for all criminal offences; and now, at last, by section 96 (2) of the Children Act 1989 when it comes into force, children are permitted to give unsworn evidence in all civil proceedings.

Section 38 of the Children and Young Persons Act 1933, which permits a young child to give unsworn evidence in criminal proceedings, allows this to be done where the court considers the child is 'of sufficient intelligence to justify the reception of the evidence, and understands the duty of speaking the truth', and section 96 (2) of the Children Act 1989 lays down a similar test for the civil courts to follow. No minimum age is laid down by these statutes, and there is little doubt that Parliament originally intended to make it in principle possible for the courts to listen to the evidence of any child, however young, provided he could talk intelligibly. In 1958, however, the Court of Criminal Appeal in the case of *Wallwork* (42 CrApR 153) decreed that it is improper for any court to receive the evidence of a child as young as five: 'The jury could not attach any value to the evidence of a child of five: it is ridiculous to suppose they could.' In the case of *Wright* (1987) 90 CrApR 91 the Court of Appeal reaffirmed this ruling, and extended it to the case where by the time of trial the child had reached the age of six.

For the disastrous results that follow from these rulings one only has to read the newspapers.

> A man charged with raping a five-year-old girl walked free from court yesterday without having to stand trial. The case collapsed after a judge decided the alleged victim was too young to give evidence...[The judge] warned the Crown Prosecution Service that in future cases it must think very carefully before bringing charges for sex offences against very young children. He then discharged without trial the man who, looking stunned, hurriedly left the court (*Glasgow Herald*, 19 May 1989).

Usually, the disastrous result produced is that a guilty man goes free; but by refusing to listen to the child the law also sometimes risks the even greater disaster of convicting someone who is innocent — as where a white man is prosecuted for assaulting a little girl of three, and the defence are precluded from putting before the court evidence that she described her attacker as black (see *Sparks v R* [1964] AC 964).

Very recently, the Court of Appeal has back-tracked from *Wallwork* and from *Wright* to the extent of saying there is no magic age below which a child is automatically disqualified from giving evidence (*B, The Times*, 1 March 1990). According to Lord Chief Justice Lane, it is up to the judge who is trying the case to decide whether the particular child in question can satisfy the test that the statute lays down. But he added his view that a child of five would come up to the required standard 'very rarely'.

In most other legal systems, including that of Scotland, the courts are willing in principle to listen to the evidence of children virtually from the age that they can talk. If this can be done north of the Tweed it is hard to think of any sane reason why we cannot do it here.

Open court

In England, the general rule is that evidence must be given live, in open court, on the day of trial, and that it must be given in the presence of the parties to the case. This makes giving evidence an ordeal for adults, let alone for children, who often find the strain considerably worse. For many years this has been partly recognised in civil proceedings, where a number of concessions to the frailty of children have been made. In care proceedings, for example, the Magistrates' Courts (Children and Young Persons) Rules empower a bench that is hearing an application for a care order to evict the child's parents from the court while the child is giving evidence. Until very recently, however, no concessions at all have been made in criminal proceedings, and it has been necessary for children called as prosecution witnesses to give their evidence live, in the presence of the accused.

When child witnesses in child abuse cases have to give their evidence in the presence of the person they accuse, the result is frequently to scare them silent. As long ago as 1925 the Departmental Committee on Sexual Offences Against Young Persons (Cmnd. 2561) said:

> We have had many cases brought to our notice in which a child or young person has been overcome with distress and fright in giving evidence at the trial and has broken down or even fainted. The result of this distress has sometimes been that no evidence could be obtained and the case has consequently been lost or has had to be withdrawn.

After years of public apathy, there was a lot of public agitation about this problem in the 1980s, with the result that two significant changes have been made.

The first is that the criminal courts have begun to allow children to give evidence from behind screens, which enable them to do so without having to see the defendant. This was first done in a trial at the Old Bailey in 1987, and the practice was eventually approved by the Court of Appeal when it affirmed the conviction of the defendants in 1989 (*X Y and Z, The Times*, 3 November 1989).

The second is that Parliament passed section 32 of the Criminal Justice Act 1988, which enables children under fourteen to give evidence in child abuse cases from an adjoining room by means of a live video link. This equipment was introduced in fourteen Crown Court centres experimentally during 1989, and it has since been made available in a further seven. Meanwhile a Home Office research team, headed by Professor Graham Davies, a psychologist with extensive experience of child witnesses, is monitoring the experiment.

From the information that has been made public to date, it seems that both screens and the live video link enable some children to give evidence successfully in cases where they would almost certainly have failed to do so without. To that extent, both devices have been successful in enabling the courts to listen to children. If these improvements manage to reduce the stress a child witness suffers in the course of giving evidence, however, they make no difference to what is thought to be an equal or even greater source of stress for them, namely the fact that they must live through many months of anxious waiting in order to give their evidence live at trial. Unlike the stress of giving evidence in court, this pre-trial stress does not show up dramatically with children collapsing in tears in the witness-box. Its effect is that cases are not brought at all, or are dropped in the early stages — something which is much less visible. As a result, many judges, barristers, press-reporters and members of the general public seem unaware of it. To those who must deal with abused children who are waiting for the trial, however, it is only too familiar.

The only way of dealing with this particular stress is to abandon any attempt to make the criminal courtroom user-friendly to child witnesses, and to go over to a system under which the evidence is officially taken in advance of trial, as is done in a large number of other legal systems. Such a change in England would not be completely unthinkable, provided the defence were given the chance to put their questions to the witness at the time the evidence was taken. Indeed, there is already in existence a procedure by which this may sometimes be done. Sections 42 and 43 of the Children and Young Persons Act 1933 provide that where a court appearance would involve serious risk to a child's life or health, a magistrate may take his evidence in advance. Then, provided the defence were given a chance to put their questions at the time the evidence was taken, a written transcript of the evidence-taking session can replace a live appearance by the child at trial. This provision, which was first enacted in a statute of 1894 as a result of campaigning efforts by the

NSPCC, is narrowly drawn, and in practice it seems to be rarely if ever used. A Home Office circular issued to the police and others in 1988 makes mention of it, however, and we may find there is some mileage in it yet.

The hearsay rule

In principle, the law does not permit a party to call witness A to say they heard non-witness B say something happened in order to establish the fact that it did happen. Either B must be produced to give live evidence to the court, or the incident must be proved by other means. The rule applies to documents as well as oral statements: witness A may not read the court a document non-witness B has written describing the event. And it also applies to tape-recordings, whether audio or video: so witness A may not play the court an audio or videotape that he has made of B describing the incident either. Furthermore, although there are many important exceptions to the hearsay rule, the fact that it is impossible to produce B to give live evidence as a witness does not automatically put it out of action.

The justification for the hearsay rule is that hearsay evidence is weak because B was not on oath and not subject to cross-examination when he told his tale to A, and because A may have changed B's tale in the retelling. This may be an acceptable reason for rejecting hearsay in a criminal case, where the evidence will be assessed by a jury of inexperienced laymen, but it is a much less acceptable reason for rejecting it in civil proceedings, where the evidence will be assessed by a judge or a magistrate who should have enough wit and experience to treat it with the appropriate degree of caution. Thus when we look at the exceptions to the hearsay rule, we find that for civil cases the list is longer, and there are a number of exceptions that are not available in the criminal courts.

At one time there was thought to be a general exception to the hearsay rule in all civil proceedings to do with the care and upbringing of children. Thus in a custody dispute, for example, or in care proceedings, the court could allow an adult — like a doctor, teacher, police officer or social worker — to repeat to the court what a young child had said. In a case in 1989, however, the Court of Appeal dropped a bombshell by holding that this was wrong, and the general power to disregard the hearsay rule in child care cases was the exclusive prerogative of the High Court in wardship (*H v H* [1989] 3 WLR 933). There was an immediate outcry against this decision, and the Government rapidly got Parliament to reverse it by inserting a last-minute amendment to the Children Bill, which is now to be found as section 96(4) of the Children Act 1989.

This section did not actually reverse the decision in *H v H*, however. It merely empowered the Lord Chancellor to make an Order reversing it. And the Order which the Lord Chancellor (or one of his officials) eventually produced does not simply reverse the decision either, but makes a series of different exceptions to it for different courts. Under the Children (Admissibility of Hearsay) Order 1990, all hearsay evidence is made admissible in child care proceedings that are heard in the High Court or the County Court; in the juvenile court department of the magistrates' court certain types of hearsay are made admissible, including hearsay accounts of what a child has said; and in the magistrates' domestic court no exceptions to the hearsay rule are made at all. This is very surprising, because the domestic court hears many custody disputes where there is an issue about whether a child has been maltreated, and the bench consists of the same type of people who staff the juvenile court. Thus there is no intelligible reason for treating the two tribunals differently. The reason for this inept and complex provision is thought to be that the Order is a compromise between the two departments which share responsibility for the magistrates' courts, namely the Lord Chancellor's Department and the Home Office, the first of which wanted a comprehensive change and the second of which wanted no change at all. The result, if an improvement on the law as it stood after *H v H*, is still unsatisfactory.

In criminal proceedings, and in those civil proceedings where it still applies, the hearsay rule combines with the competency requirement to shut the ears of the court to what a large number of children have to say. Where the child is very young the competency requirement prevents the court from listening to the child in person — and the hearsay rule prevents the court from listening to an adult's account of what the child has said.

Rules about corroboration

If the three rules just mentioned make it difficult for the courts to listen to children, then, in a criminal case, the rules about corroboration sometimes add to the problem by requiring the court to take little notice of what the children have to say.

Before 1988 the corroboration rules were as follows. (1) There could be no conviction on the unsworn evidence of a child unless it was corroborated, and corroborated by something other than more unsworn evidence of other children. Thus if the prosecution had no witnesses to the offence other than a group of children, all of whom were too immature to 'understand the nature of an oath', the judge would be obliged to stop the case. (2) Where any child gave evidence, even on oath, the judge was bound to direct the jury that it

9   Persuading the courts to listen to children   119

was 'dangerous' to act on the evidence of a child without corroboration, and was obliged to do this not only where there was no corroboration of the child's story, but — absurdly — even where there was obviously ample corroboration, and even where the judge thought there was really no danger at all in accepting the evidence of this particular child.

During the 1980s it became accepted that these rules disparaged the evidence of children unnecessarily, and by section 34 of the Criminal Justice Act 1988 they were both abolished. The change is less significant than appears, however, because there remains in existence an independent rule of criminal evidence that in a sex case the judge must always warn the jury of the danger of accepting the uncorroborated evidence of a sexual complainant. As children, when they give evidence in criminal proceedings, very commonly do so as victims of sexual offences, the same sort of corroboration warning must frequently be given, although for a different reason.

Reform in sight? The proposals of the Pigot Committee

When the Criminal Justice Bill was before Parliament there was public pressure for changes to the rules about children's evidence more radical than those the Bill contained, and in particular, pressure to make videotapes of previous interviews with children admissible in criminal child abuse prosecutions. To meet this pressure the Government set up an advisory group chaired by the Common Serjeant, Judge Tom Pigot, QC, to investigate the possible wider use of video evidence in trials where children and other vulnerable witnesses were involved. The report of this advisory group — usually referred to as the Pigot Committee — was published in December 1989.[2] The proposals it contains would go a long way to make it easier for the courts to listen to children.

As far as the competency requirement is concerned, the Pigot Committee is in favour of abolishing it completely. In the Committee's opinion, the court should be willing to listen to the evidence of any child who is capable of communicating intelligibly. They say that a child's immaturity should affect the weight that the court gives to its evidence, but should not prevent the court hearing it at all, as is the case at present.

As for the corroboration rules, or what is left of them, the Pigot Committee recommends that they should be abolished too. In their view, it is sufficient that the judge should have a discretionary power to give the jury such a warning — if any — he thinks the totality of evidence in the case requires.

As far as the 'open court' rules are concerned, the Pigot

Committee proposes a new scheme under which the evidence of children would routinely be taken in advance of trial. In any case where a child appears to be a witness to an incident of sex or violence, they propose that the child should be examined in informal surroundings by a trained child examiner, operating under an official Code of Practice, and that this examination should be videotaped. As soon as practicable thereafter this tape should be shown to the suspect at a police station, in order to obtain his reaction to it. It should then be shown to a judge, who would have a discretionary power to rule it inadmissible in evidence if he thought that because of the way the child had been questioned, or for other reasons, it would be more prejudicial than probative to allow it to be used at trial. If the judge thought the tape acceptable, he would then order a preliminary hearing in his chambers attended by the lawyers for the prosecution and the defence, the child, and the child's 'support person'. At this preliminary hearing the child would be shown the tape of the earlier interview, the prosecuting lawyer would ask a few introductory questions, and the defendant's lawyer would be given the chance to put his or her questions to the child. While this hearing was taking place the defendant would not be physically present, but would be able to watch and hear the proceedings through a one-way mirror or live TV link, and to communicate with his lawyer through a microphone and earpiece. This preliminary hearing, like the first interview, would be recorded on videotape. At the eventual trial the videotape of the first interview would replace the child's evidence in-chief, and the videotape of the preliminary hearing would replace the traditional in-court cross-examination. By this means, the Pigot Committee believes the court would be able to receive the evidence of many children who are unable to communicate by giving evidence in open court, it would obtain fuller and more coherent evidence from those children who are able to give some evidence by the traditional method, and that the child would be relieved of the long and agonising wait to give live evidence at trial. The result should be better justice for everyone, including the innocent defendant, and less stress for the child.

    A problem that worried the Pigot Committee was the child who is too young or too disturbed to communicate with the lawyers who would be conducting the preliminary hearing. By a majority, they propose that the judge should have power to order the advocates to put their questions through a person approved by the court who enjoys the confidence of the child. This provoked the sole dissent in the Report: from Anne Rafferty, a barrister, who felt the proper solution was to allow the advocates a chance to talk informally to the child before the trial, in order to 'break the ice'.

    The Pigot Committee does not recommend any further changes

in the hearsay rule, a matter which it thought would take it too far beyond its terms of reference. However, its main proposal, if introduced, would make it much easier for the court in criminal proceedings to listen directly to the child, and so reduce the pressure to receive a hearsay account.

Conclusion

It is likely that Britain will soon sign and ratify the United Nations Convention on the Rights of the Child. Among other obligations, this Convention imposes on the contracting States the duty to give children an opportunity to be heard in all legal proceedings that affect them, and the duty to see that appropriate measures are taken to ensure the physical and psychological recovery of children who are victims of abuse, ill-treatment or neglect. Until we have removed the various impediments that prevent the courts in England listening to children, the United Kingdom will hardly be able to accede to the Convention with an easy mind.

References

1. Waugh, R. (1913) *The Life of Benjamin Waugh*, London: T. Fisher Unwin.
2. *The Report of the Advisory Group on Video Evidence* (1989) (Pigot Committee). ISBN 0 86252 478 4. (Available from the Home Office, but not from HMSO.)

Part 4
Therapy for the abused child

10 Listening to, talking to and understanding children — reality, imagination, dreams and fantasy

Judith Trowell

Introduction

In retrospect it seems strange, almost bizarre, that we have had to reach almost the end of the twentieth century before listening to children, before talking to children, has seemed important. Why has it taken so long? We have all been children, how far back we can remember varies but we have all been there, we all know the impact external events and relationships and our own dreams, thoughts, hopes and fears had on us. And yet we have until quite recently not seen the need — professionally at least — to talk to children and to really try and hear them, understand their communications. It has only really become discussable in the latter half of this century. The underlying issues of power, of status, must be for others to explore. The recognition of children as people, as individuals with personalities, minds, memories, growing and evolving but nonetheless with their own individuality, their own identity, is what interests me, and the reflection that adults must have chosen not to see them as such for their own reasons. What adults have done with and to children has to be part of the answer, and if no-one wanted to think about it and the implications, then it can't have been very 'nice' a lot of the time or why were adults ashamed? Physical abuse, physical neglect, emotional abuse, emotional neglect, sexual abuse, spring to mind at once.

Child and Family Mental Health Services have as part of their core skills 'Listening to and Communicating with Children'. However, there has been a reluctance to become involved in abuse work, perhaps because when working with abused children one must be capable of moving from one domain to another engaging in different discourses. The discourse most relevant is the Child Protection discourse. Anyone listening to children needs to be able to think about what he or she is hearing, using these perspectives and able to move from one to another aware of what he or she is doing.

Are Child Protection issues coming up in the material, do I need to do anything, inform anyone? The legal discourse sometimes feels like an imposition because from this perspective one has to consider the questions being asked and the responses from the child, verbal, non-verbal and behavioural. Will it be possible to use this as evidence in court? I must be careful not to say or do anything that will be prejudiced or discount what is emerging in this interaction with the child. When doing an assessment for the court the parameters are clear but only too often abuse emerges as an issue after prolonged contact with a child, e.g. a child who is neglected or physically abused begins to disclose sexual abuse.

The therapeutic discourse is easier, although it may be extraordinarily painful, but the aim of providing relief from distress is clear, dealing with the range of feelings — rage, hate, guilt, shame, excitement, power, helplessness, hopelessness, love, joy, hope, despair — and helping children make sense of his or her experiences. The confusion, bewilderment, mixed messages, the gaps, the losses, the rejections — whether the work is slow or rapid, is sustained by seeing the child move forward, gradually integrate his or her experiences and begin to be a person rather than an object, with feelings and capacities, capable of making satisfying relationships. This part of listening to children has its own rewards.

The research discourse requires that one is constantly thinking, reflecting on what is being said or done. Could it be done better? Are there other more effective strategies? Is the time being spent listening to this child time well spent? We must evaluate the intervention and be aware of alternatives if good practise is to remain good.

Definitions of abuse

1. Physical abuse occurs where any child under the age of seventeen years is injured and the nature of the injury is not

consistent with the account of how it occurred, or where there is definite knowledge or reasonable suspicion that the injury was inflicted or not knowingly prevented by any person having custody, charge or care of the child. This includes children to whom it is suspected poisonous substances have been administered.

This latter may be seen as physical abuse, but it may be part of a 'Münchhausen by Proxy Syndrome', e.g. when sugar is added deliberately to urine samples by a carer and a child is intensively investigated for diabetes, or blood is added to a nappy and the child is investigated for rectal or colonic bleeds. Other children are trailed from hospital to hospital for investigations, operations etc.; the physical abuse is carried out by unsuspecting health care professionals trying to do their job as thoroughly as possible, but the true abuser is the carer who is seeking attention.

2. Physical neglect occurs where children under seventeen years of age have been persistently or severely neglected, for example by exposure to dangers, cold, starvation.
3. Emotional abuse occurs:
    a) where children under seventeen years of age have been medically diagnosed as suffering from severe non-organic failure to thrive; the signs of this are dwarfism, cold and pink hands and feet, compliant attitude and body (for example if a child is asked to take up a position or moved into one the posture is maintained until he or she is told to move), feeding disorder, language delay, low intelligence with delay in development, an inability to play, behaviour disorder with enuresis or encopresis and attachment disorder with severe separation anxiety or detached and indifferent behaviour;
    b) where behaviour and emotional development have been severely affected, where medical and social assessments find evidence of either persistent or severe neglect and/or rejection. This can be complemented by a statement about a child's basic needs which give guidelines and help define emotional abuse:

    i. Physical care and protection
    ii. Affection and approval
    iii. Stimulation and teaching
    iv. Discipline and control which is consistent and age-appropriate
    v. Opportunity and encouragement to gradually acquire autonomy

This latter highlights the abusive nature of the over-protective,

suffocating caretaker who can't allow the child to separate and individuate, or have its own thoughts and feelings.
4. Sexual abuse still lacks a nationally and internationally agreed definition although the Kempe (Schechter and Roberge 1976)[1] definition is widely used (DOH). Sexual abuse is defined as the involvement of dependent developmentally immature children and adolescents in sexual activity that they do not fully comprehend and to which they are unable to give informed consent, or that violates the social taboos of family roles. When listening to children this is not very useful in predicting the degree of distress and disturbance and the Mrazek and Mrazek[2] definition is more helpful in its use of general broad categories:

   i.   Exposure (viewing of sexual acts, pornography and exhibitionism)
   ii. Molestation (fondling of genitals of children or adults)
   iii. Sexual intercourse (oral, vaginal or anal)
   iv. Rape (acute or chronic assaultative forced intercourse)

   This definition is also helpful in separating out passive sexual abuse (no contact) (i) from active sexual abuse (contact) (ii), (iii) and (iv).
5. Grave concern is in fact the most frequently used category for registration, 41% of those on 88/89 (March 31st) register (DOH). Grave concern implies there was considerable anxiety and suspicion but nothing clear-cut. Children in this category may have considerable difficulties and need help, but listening to these children requires particular attention to the discourse.

The child in context

In order to be able to hear a child, i.e. to listen and to take in and then make sense of the child and its communication, it is generally helpful to have some understanding of the child's context. If time permits and the situation is not too extreme or urgent, it is helpful to see the child in the family in which it is living, the child and the caretakers and any siblings, i.e. all the people living under one roof. It is often very useful too to see the child with its sibling group without the adults. If the child is in nursery, playgroup or school nursery class, primary or secondary school, it is very helpful if someone has observed the child in this setting.

It is perhaps worthwhile elaborating on the idea of observing. Observing family and child interaction is a particular skill that needs to be learnt. The capacity to observe involves being able to be with whoever is being observed and to have part of oneself interacting, whilst at the same time looking, watching and monitoring what is going on. Not only what is said, but the looks, glances, eye contacts, the body movements, hand and finger movements, body posture, touches, pats, hugs, physical closeness, or lack of it, physical restraints, however subtle, with which one human being controls another. The monitoring also extends to oneself: part of the capacity to observe is recording one's own reactions, using oneself as an instrument to pick up nonverbal or unconscious communications so that these too can be used to understand what is occurring. In order to do this we need a considerable degree of self knowledge, because it is essential not to confuse one's own responses due to one's own emotional baggage, with anything arising from the child or family.

The setting

A child needs to feel comfortable in the room where he or she is seen, so consideration needs to be given to the size and atmosphere of the room and to ensure there are not unnecessary interruptions. Suitable play and drawing materials need to be available and attractively set out.

Meeting the child

When with children the difficulty in communication and listening to children can be obvious — the language barrier or more subtle use of words. Children communicate verbally and non-verbally by their body posture, their mood, the feelings they provoke in those around and by their actions, play, drawing, gait, behaviour. In order to make sense of all these modes of communication we have to be open to all the forms of communication, knowing that there is also a developmental continuum. A sound knowledge of child development, body, intellect, mind, personality and psychosexual development is important.

Seeing a child alone is not easy, does not come naturally and raises considerable anxiety. Many adults are afraid to be with a child alone. What do you say? How do you behave? Can an adult male be in a room alone with a child?

Depending on the age of the child and how long they can cope with being with you, a relative stranger, it is important to have two sorts of experiences; they can either be in two separate meetings or can run consecutively in one interview. However, it is extremely important *not* to have meetings that are too lengthy. After one and a half hours to two hours a child will be past it and anything discovered will be suspect. It is preferable to have two meetings of less than an hour each.

Unstructured period

The child is shown what is available in the way of play materials. It is helpful to explain what the child may or may not do and that the expectation is that the toys will remain at the end of the meeting in the room.

If the child is hesitant or nervous play can be facilitated, and if after one activity the child is at a loss, several options can be indicated to the child. If the child becomes very actively engaged in play, it might be appropriate to ask him or her to tell you what is happening, what it is all about, e.g. 'I was wondering what was going on?' or, 'Can you tell me about...the drawing, the plasticine, the model.'

Older children and adolescents may not play but instead will just sit. It should be possible to engage young people if you ask why they think they have had to come, and then by indicating interest in them, their school, their homes, the music they like, TV programmes, sports.

The aim at whatever age is to have obtained a view on how the child thinks, functions when there is no specific task, how much the child can explore ideas, or play materials, how creative the child is, how free they are in themselves i.e. some view on their confidence, self-esteem. If children have been threatened or subjected to violence they may constantly need to ask permission, check the interviewer's response, even ask directly for approval. Some children may seek close physical contact, want to sit on the interviewer's lap or be sexually aware. Other children may be completely self-contained and make no reference to and have no contact with the interviewer at all. If a child is making a model or busily playing and it goes wrong, how they deal with frustration and difficulty is instructive. Can they persevere, do they give up or do they smash the whole thing in rage?

Structured period

In the second meeting, or the second half of the longer meeting, a more structured approach needs to be used. Certain areas need to be explored. There may be concern about what has been going on at home or at school, and this must be raised.

Specific topics to cover include bad dreams and nightmares, frightening or upsetting incidents, events, people; moves and changes of caretaker, who sleeps where, and with whom. Friends, school and changes of school, relationships with teachers, who you talk to if you are frightened and upset, who you talk to if you are happy, excited, day dreams, pretend imaginings, three wishes, fun, excitement, who with, doing what? What you enjoy, do well at school, what you dislike. I ask all children about cuddles, hugs and who has touched or stroked them? The anatomically correct dolls could come in as part of this, helping a child to express something they find hard to put into words or giving them the opportunity to express feelings about key figures in their lives, extended family and family friends included.

I explore the use of alcohol and drugs and from eight to nine years up ask whether life is worth living, and discuss suicidal thoughts and any actions.

Pets and favourite toys can be revealing; some children may give and receive more affection from a pet than any other living thing and toys may be key as confidantes and for cuddles.

As a psychiatrist I specifically have to consider the mental state of the child and whether there is developmental delay. Over the last few years I have seen more seriously disturbed children than ever before. Many of these children have been involved in sexual abuse or are members of families where sexual abuse has been going on. These disturbed children may be very difficult to contain in the room, running all over the place, trying to climb out of the window with no sense of danger. If I ask why they are doing these things they talk about being a superhero figure and this protects them against a range of terrifying or attacking images that they may see or hear or both, or feeling very small and helpless. There may be times when they believe all this to be true and real, i.e. they lose touch with reality. Developmental delay reveals itself in an inability to play in an age appropriate way, problems with speech, with co-ordinating, with learning, with feeding and sphincter control. It frequently occurs as the result of abuse. Developmentally delayed children are also vulnerable to further abuse.

Understanding the communications of children

The purpose of all that has gone before is to enable us, the adults, to understand as much as we can.

Seeing a child in its natural family or with the substitute caregivers, or both where appropriate, enables one to be aware of the family myths, the family stories that are used to explain and justify various behaviours. Cultural and class variables emerge which it is important to be aware of before arriving at any conclusions. The family dynamics can usually be glimpsed, the power structures, the pairings or subsystems, the boundaries or lack of them, the intergenerational influences. More subtle and difficult to pick up are the expectations, the beliefs, the behaviours that this family tolerates or considers unacceptable.

The relationships between the children and between the child and the parents are extremely important to observe. Often nonverbal communication can give clues that lead to possibilities that might otherwise have been missed.

Seeing the child in a setting outside the family can be illuminating. The child may behave in a similar way or may be dramatically different. For example, the crushed scapegoated child at home may be defiant, aggressive and difficult.

Some children for a variety of reasons are closed over, shut in and it is extremely difficult to make contact. Often young people have turned their backs on adults for a range of reasons; even more worrying is if they have cut themselves off from their peer group as well. I may suggest they can direct any film they like, providing the plot themselves or using an existing play or film they know. Asking a psychologist to see the young person to use psychometric and projective tests can be a useful way of making contact.

Most children and young people welcome the chance to play and talk and have an adult's undivided attention. Those that have been subjected to threats are also keen to be with you but there are gaps, lacunae that make contact with them patchy and disconcerting with inconsistencies.

To understand what children are saying we need to look at the context, to understand their notion of time and realise that their use of language may differ from ours. In order to listen more effectively to children they have to be given time, in the right sort of setting, and the person listening needs to be able to make sense of and be open to what the child is communicating. As suggested earlier, a particularly good way of helping workers develop these skills is an observational training.

The worker learns:

1. about early child development
2. about preverbal and nonverbal communication
3. about cultural and gender issues and how these are transmitted
4. about parenting skills and sibling relationships
5. about how children use primary and secondary attachment figures
6. above all about how to observe — really see — what is going on whilst interacting in the here and now, whilst reflecting, thinking about these and becoming aware of what they know and don't know.

7. to suspend judgement, not make cause/effect decisions, but having collected the raw 'data' then try and understand, using the range of theoretical perspectives — learning theory, systems theory, attachment theory, psychodynamic theory
8. to see how they are dominated by preconceptions and assumptions

If the training group is observing children with a range of cultures and backgrounds in a range of settings, the learning experience is greatly enriched. Observing a child and hearing other observations is also an excellent way of developing skills in communicating with children. The observer sees and hears caretakers and other children interacting and with the range discussed in the seminar begins to build up a vocabulary, a language, to use when they need to listen to and then communicate *with* children.

Physical abuse, neglect, emotional abuse and sexual abuse usually leave the child emotionally damaged and their personality and development distorted — whether the damage to their physical body was severe or not. Listening to these children and understanding them means exposing oneself to the mental and emotional pain the child is experiencing. It also may reawaken memories and feelings from one's own childhood and also how one functioned as a parent with one's own children. Both of these may be very distressing. It is vital that the child client does not become caught in, enmeshed in the worker's personal background, their own emotional life. Each worker needs to be aware of this and have ways of dealing with their own feelings before children have begun to trust them enough and before the worker has begun to offer children that precious gift of really listening to what they are saying.

Particular issues and examples

Physical abuse

All children's play and drawings can be seen as a communication. The basis may be real experience (the child re-enacts an event to try and make sense of it), or they may be less direct and events may be played out in a disguised form. Or the play may depict fantasy, the child's imagination generating the ideas. An imaginative creative child may take material from stories, TV, videos and weave them into pretend play and there may or may not be a real component to it. It is not easy to unravel, and violence is one of the two difficult areas (the second being sexuality). The child may have been subjected to violence, may have witnessed violence, may have seen a terrifying TV programme or the News, read a story or have had a nightmare or daydream they can't make sense of. We all, including children, have violent angry destructive feelings that we are afraid of and fearful we cannot control. We are all, also, aware of our own anger, fearful of the violence locked up in those around us.

Andrew was a physically abused child; his mother complained he was out of control, unmanageable. He was six years old. She agreed she had hit him on many occasions and she accepted his name being on the Child Protection Register. The school also reported that he was out of control, violent with other children, an extremely difficult child. He was seen with his family and then he was seen alone.

It was not an easy meeting: he was not a child one responded to with warmth. He was well dressed and well spoken but he had cuts — or scratches — on his face and hand and a bruise on his left cheek. He started to draw but rapidly gave up. He messed with the plasticine and them pulled a lump into quite a good cow, he showed me and then slammed it down so that it was flattened. He spent the rest of the time throwing and kicking a ball he took out of his pocket. He built up the force with which he kicked the ball so that I was fearful for myself and the room but he was well coordinated and had good reactions and nothing was damaged. He talked about various people and I took pen and paper and tried to sort out who all the people were and their relationships. It was not clear whether he was confused or whether he chose not to give me information. He talked about his cousins and various cohabitees.

When I asked something he quite often ignored me so I became increasingly irritated and felt cut off, out of touch with him or couldn't he hear me? I wondered about his hearing, was he deaf?

Eye contact was minimal but he did respond to a question about nightmares. Yes, he did have bad dreams, that monsters or something in the dark were coming to attack him, kill him. He went on to tell me he had been hit, attacked by his mother (he used her first name). He said he was very angry with her. He repeated this several times in a cold hard voice. When I asked if he ever had felt upset or hurt, there was no response, I was ignored. He repeated that he would never forgive her, or forget she was bad. He answered very cursorily about his younger sister, where she was when Mum hit him.

I was relieved when the meeting ended. I felt I was with an ice cube. Would it melt or was there nothing but deadness? The expression on his face with the cow and when talking about mother and sister and when he looked at me (a woman) was hard and cruel but also the excitement, pleasure and triumph when the ball whizzed past me and my eyes must have registered the anxiety I felt, was very worrying.

This boy shows quite well how he is coping with his pain, he denies it exists except at night but people around experience the physical pain (when hit) and the anxiety. His hearing test had been normal.

I think Andrew shows how the physical abuse has distorted his emotional development. The violence at school, the cold dismissal of his mother and the threats to me with the ball indicate how he has coped by developing his aggressive controlling omnipotent side.

The vulnerable loving needy side has been pushed away, but does emerge a little in the nightmares. The price for this coping strategy is high however. Creativity is non-existent, he was not learning in school, could not read or write, and he had no warm relationships, he wasn't likeable.

Neglect

When keeping warm and trying to find enough to eat the child may become very self sufficient and self reliant or may become listless, apathetic, detached and dejected.

Aged eight, Sally was a rather pathetic looking child in ill-fitting skimpy clothes and she looked thin and peaky. Her mother was known to be preoccupied and depressed, unable to cope with her family and home. The children had come into care because of failure to gain weight and height and poor attendance at school. Sally had to care for her three younger siblings and had tried to keep the home going. She was doing very badly with schoolwork.

Sally came easily with me and told me at once she wanted to paint. We spent time finding the colours she wanted, she persevered in the search. She became engrossed in painting a vast amount of blue — blue sky and a bright yellow sun, green hills with a house and a tree and a signpost. When the paint ran or smudged she accepted it with a resigned fatalism as though she were powerless, nothing she could do would alter the course of events. In fact she could have prevented the picture from being damaged or spoilt. It was hard not to intervene and show how the drips could be caught and stopped. Once it was spoilt, she worked very hard trying to repair it. She stayed with the picture, working hard, concentrating and persisting. She added a few grey clouds and then kept repeating that it was no good, she was useless. It felt very sad.

It seemed to me she had no sense of worth, her self-esteem was very low, she had no idea that she had the capacity to produce anything good or worthwhile.

She told me that a lot of the time she feels odd, strange, sort of fed-up and miserable. She felt that a lot at school, at home it was better. She never wants to go to school and most of the time worries about Mum — is she all right, and when there every day she used to worry, will Mum be there when I get home from school? She said she found school difficult, that she is thick, stupid, doesn't understand things. She is usually thinking about Mum anyway. At times she said she was frightened of Mum, although not sure quite why, just never sure what Mum might do. Mum gets very angry at times. I asked if she herself ever got angry, she looked annoyed and said no.

Sally was rather a sad vulnerable child. She was quite responsible with her younger siblings but had no sense of being provided for, parented and no sense of any good things inside herself or available for her.

Sally's individuality and identity have not been validated; she has also not been cared for practically. She has coped by managing to find things for herself and then by parenting her younger siblings has had some warmth and affection. Any sense of expecting to be cared for wasn't there, and her emotional development is quite distorted. Appropriate assertiveness and anger is pushed away, her creativity is there a little, the wistful house with blue sky and sunshine, but the forlorn sadness is powerful.

Any mental energy for learning is not there; guilt, hopelessness and despair are overwhelming. Physically she was frail with hair and skin that looked unhealthy and uncared for.

Emotional abuse

Emotional abuse is rather difficult to prove unless it is really extreme. It is, however, very important, and the emotionally abusive component of physical and sexual abuse is probably what produces the lasting damage. To be subjected to contempt, derision, criticism, unrealistic expectations or hatred, or have your existence denied and be totally ignored and rejected leads to a loss of personality development, a loss of self esteem, to intense self-doubt, an inability to have thoughts and ideas of one's own. When feelings are never validated or reciprocated the individual can fragment in a sea of uncertainty or become cold and feelingless.

Ruth was twelve years old; she had been kept in the kitchen and had not eaten with the rest of the family, she was expected to do a lot of the jobs around the house and although her siblings had pocket money she had none. At night she was locked in her bedroom from 8 pm to 7.30 am.

Ruth agreed that life at home had been difficult. She thought it had been right to take her into care. It had been very bad at home at that time, it was better now. She is enjoying school for the first time and has some friends, she is finding she can learn. She is in some trouble though because she chats to her friends and the teachers tell her off. There was a great deal of eye contact and yet I felt distanced, her eyes seemed to fasten on me but not really see me, engage with me — they slid to one side if I looked back. She kept her coat buttoned up and I felt shut out. She gave me brief smiles but when I looked at her when she was preoccupied with her own thoughts, she was unaware of my glance, then she looked sad and watchful. There was no sense of fun, pleasure, vitality, just a need to be very careful. She several times told me the situation was much better. She was forlorn and isolated and yet I didn't feel particularly sympathetic. I could have easily told her to get on and do — whatever — draw. I asked if she talked to anyone when she was upset or angry and she insisted no-one, she keeps it inside herself. I asked if she talked to or felt closer to the animals. She said no, she walked the dog and cleaned out the rabbit, but didn't really cuddle or talk to any of them.

Ruth was a very sad vulnerable child but instead of feeling sympathetic it would have been easy to be irritated and urge her to get on and do something as though she had no ideas of her own, no initiative.

Ruth shows how without encouragement, without validation, and particularly if everything one is, one says, and one does is rejected, the personality goes into retreat.

It almost felt as if any response, for example ordering her to do something, was better than being in the free unstructured situation with me. Although there were play materials she could not — would not dare — to do something, draw something. Somehow she would get it wrong inevitably.

Sexual abuse

Sexuality is more complex than aggression. We are all sexual beings but explicit sexual knowledge is acquired gradually. Why is it more difficult to unravel? Perhaps it is because of our own problem with language and our own emotional responses that the children pick up. It is important to have a good understanding of psychosexual development. Unless there is a good knowledge of how boys and girls establish their gender identity and their sexual orientation and the different phases all normal children pass through, it is hard to be sure one is clear about normality and abnormality. Where the child is in its psychosexual development also has a considerable bearing on the impact on the child of child sexual abuse. Children are full of fantasies, about how babies are made, what different parts of the male and female body are precisely used for, and these thoughts slowly become clarified. Sexual abuse imposes reality on the child before they have had the mental and emotional space to do all the digesting and work that is normally part of growing up. In addition the threats and secrecy that usually go with sexual abuse mean that the child is left feeling confused, dirty, angry, ashamed and embarrassed if their body responded and participated in the sexual activity. The damage to the child's development is therefore particularly destructive and it penetrates to the core of the personality.

Lucy, aged four and a half years, was a sexually abused child where there had been vaginal and anal intercourse since she was about a year old. She was in foster care, her mother had a mental breakdown and was in a mental hospital following the discovery of the abuse. Father was serving a period in prison.

Her foster mother told me she had 'found Lucy difficult, you can't get through to her, feel in contact with her, although she is physically there.' Lucy didn't show any affection to anyone.

On her own Lucy didn't play with the animals, dolls or plasticine, she scribbled a little but then spent the time doing the jigsaw. This meant that Lucy pointed to a piece and I had to suggest the next piece to it. She had reasonable manual dexterity and co-ordination in putting them together, but could not 'see' the next piece herself. As she did the jigsaw she talked about school and what she did there and the foster home and Mummy. I tried to clarify this and she repeatedly called her natural mother Jane and her foster mother Mummy. Lucy told me Jane was ill and couldn't look after her, sometimes she was in hospital but even when Jane wasn't she wouldn't be well enough to look after her. I asked if she felt sad about this; there was no response. When I repeated my comment she said she saw Jane for visits and that was OK but not to live with; Daddy was different. I asked about Daddy and she talked on and on about Daddy until I felt quite bewildered. I clarified she meant her own father, not foster father. Lucy explained she often sees him, talks to him. I asked about frightening or worrying things and she didn't respond, until I said what about bedtime, nighttime, any bad dreams? The rest of the time was filled by Lucy talking about monsters that came to her room to hit her, not in the night when she is asleep but when she is awake, they come and hide under her bed. Daddy is there and he protects her, he frightens them away but they keep coming back. Daddy comes every evening and in the daytime too, because the monsters come in the garden and in the house. They don't come to school. The monsters didn't come to her room. She went on and on about monsters hitting her, beating her up and Daddy protecting her.

During this account she looked at me, was very much in contact with me, animated and frightened. When the adults returned, Lucy was gone, she was again cut off, unavailable. By the end of the interview the descriptions by Lucy were so vivid that I had become convinced she was still seeing her father. I needed to check reality with her social worker and discovered he was indeed inside prison and there was no access. She was seeing her natural mother, brought from mental hospital to Social Services for access. Lucy was coping, just, but her fantasy world and reality were spilling into each other and her confusion was very apparent. What had gone on between her and her father was unthinkable for Lucy.

Hannah, eleven years old, was living with her mother and younger half-siblings; her stepfather was out of the family, on probation, and her mother wanted to get a divorce. Hannah was a parentified child, caring for her mother and younger siblings. She was quite lively and talkative, an attractive girl with dark eyes. She spoke with warmth about her grandmother (to whom the sexual abuse had been disclosed). She became quite tearful as she talked of the sexual abuse but there was a strange quality to it, I did not feel sadness. She explained step-Dad had touched her since she was five or six years old, she tried to tell her Mum when she was eight but Mum had told her Dad would never do things like that and when she tried again Mum wouldn't listen. Her step-Dad touched her and she touched him. She described mutual masturbation. She became upset when I produced the anatomically correct dolls, not wanting the male doll's trousers removed and urging me to put them away. She explained Dad hadn't gone inside her, not her mouth or anus or vagina, but she felt bad, dirty, smelly, she felt sure people could smell it on her. Dad put his thing between her legs. She felt people looked at her, she spends her time watching TV so she doesn't have to remember. At school she is all right as long as there is no time to think, remember. By now she looked a sad unhappy little girl. There seemed to be little pleasure or fun in her life. She looked horrified when I asked about boys or wondered how she saw the future. She absolutely refused to contemplate ever having boyfriends, a husband, a family. There was no rage or anger, just a passive hopeless helpless feeling. However, she was quite definite and determined about what she would and would not do when with her mother, expecting to be able to do what Hannah wanted. Hannah was physically adolescent, well into puberty, but she was either the person in charge or a very vulnerable little girl, there was no tentative pubertal curiosity or day dreams. The most striking experience was her cut-off quality, my feelings were very strong, hers were so low key.

These examples are not extreme, they were not major psychiatric problems, they are abused children who need listening to, who need to communicate their experiences, gradually make sense of them and the implications for their lives, and to try again to establish trust and hope that there are people that can hear, can understand, can bear to think and feel. Hopefully this will enable the children to be able to think and feel, bear the pain and discover the joy of living.

References

1. Schechter, Marshall, D. and Roberge, Leo, 'Sexual Exploitation' in Ray E. Helfer and C. Henry Kempe, *Child Abuse and Neglect: the family and the community*. Cambridge, Mass., Ballinger, 1976, pp 127-42.
2. Mrazek, D. A. and Mrazek, P. B. (1981) chapter in Mrazek, P. B. and Kempe, H. *Sexually Abused Children and their Families*, Pergamon.

11 'Why should I talk to you?' — Initial interviews with distressed adolescents

Paul Holmes

Terry, a well built black boy of fifteen, sat opposite me in my office looking very sullen and rather distressed. Our meeting had started with a silence which I broke:

'I get the strong feeling that you really don't wish to be here this morning.'

'Quite right, I didn't want to see you. Why should I see a shrink? Why should I say anything?'

At least Terry had said something!

At times sullen silence, or a rapid flight from my office (my shortest interview so far with an adolescent lasted 30 seconds!) are the responses I receive when I try to talk with a frightened, angry and perhaps abused adolescent.

I felt that Terry and I had made a start in our meeting and that progress was possible.

This chapter is about my first meetings with adolescents. My task varies: sometimes I have been asked to undertake a psychiatric assessment, at other times I am assessing the young person with the view to offering treatment.

This account is personal, based upon my work as a consultant

11 'Why should I talk to you?'

adolescent psychiatrist working in the community in inner London. I am, however, not just talking about the process of formal psychiatric or psychotherapy assessments. I hope that much of what I have to say in this chapter will be relevant to what happens when any professional meets with an adolescent for the first (and indeed subsequent) times. With less disturbed young people meetings will be more ordinary, relaxed and straightforward. I am often surprised, on meeting the offspring of friends, family and colleagues, how easy it is to talk to many teenagers; how different they are, in some ways, from the distressed young people who enter my office. In other ways, however, all teenagers are going through the same developmental stages, with more or less ease, grace and success.

When I first meet with an adolescent boy or girl, he or she has often been sent (or more usually brought) to see me by a concerned social worker, teacher or parent wanting help and advice from me on the young person whom they feel is confused and distressed. The teenagers didn't ask to see a 'shrink'. At times they fear the magical insights they assume I have into their minds, which are often muddled or tormented, and into their secrets, which can be alarming both to themselves and to others. The abused young people will have developed many defences in an attempt to cope with cruel events of their short lives. Initially my attempts to get them to talk may be experienced as yet another brutal assault on their persons and their self esteem. Words can feel as threatening and as painful as physical blows. Naturally the young people will do all they can to protect themselves from further distress.

> Terry was living with a foster family following yet another crisis at home. His parents had been separated for years, his mother (who tended to drink to excess) lived with a new partner, James, who when drunk hit her and her children. In previous crises Terry had gone to stay with his father, but this time he had once more been admitted to the local psychiatric hospital with another psychotic breakdown. Terry's foster parents were worried and rather annoyed with the boy. He wouldn't talk to them. He hid in his room. After a recent row, he had smashed up what few possessions he had, throwing the remains out of his bedroom window at passers-by. And at times they heard Terry talking to himself.
>
> 'Is he mad, like his father?' they asked Mary, his long-suffering social worker.
>
> Mary didn't know, but she'd known this family for several years and had become increasingly worried about the children, especially young Terry, who often seemed isolated and withdrawn. So she asked me if I'd see Terry for an assessment interview.

This chapter will look at some of the techniques I use when talking to distressed teenagers such as Terry. A particular focus will be the ways in which I use myself and in particular my own feelings and associations in these interviews. Some of these techniques have been developed from those I learned in my training and work in individual psychoanalytic psychotherapy. However I must emphasise that in this chapter I am talking about initial and assessment interviews *not* psychotherapy with adolescents (although many of my comments will be relevant to this process too).

Mary was very concerned about Terry's mental health. His behaviour was becoming increasingly odd, and moreover (and this was of great concern to the social worker) his foster parents were beginning to hint that they might not be able to keep Terry in their family for much longer. They felt very frustrated and at times angry with him.

So, at the very start of my first meeting with Terry, I have a dilemma: who is my client? Is it Terry, the distressed angry teenager, or is it Mary, his worried and over-worked social worker? Or, indeed, is it his foster parents?

In the classical medical or social work model I should see Terry as my client or patient. Those around him are available to provide support or information about the boy, but Terry is my patient whom it is my task (and duty) to attempt to help. In my experience, however, the situation is rarely that simple. It was the social worker who asked me for help with Terry, not the boy himself. I believe that it is possible, through the process of assessing his difficulties and needs, to offer Terry help directly (perhaps by providing counselling sessions) *and* indirectly through increasing his social worker's (and the foster parents') understanding of this troubled (and troublesome) lad.

I knew that, in a busy life, I could only see Terry a few times, even if he agreed to see me again. However his social worker saw him every day! I have discovered that I can provide indirect help to the disturbed or distressed adolescent (through meetings with the support of those in regular contact with the teenager) which can be more effective than my offering regular meetings with the adolescent — sessions that many adolescents tend to miss or avoid! I find that I can often be most useful to these other adults, and thus indirectly to the teenager, if I have met the young person at least once. However, this process requires great delicacy when actually meeting the adolescent for the first time. Issues of boundaries and confidentiality are of great importance and must be clarified with all concerned. Indeed I find it helpful that my first contact (in these circumstances) with the adolescent should be (at least for a while) together with the parents or social worker who made the referral to me. In such a

11 'Why should I talk to you?'

meeting, which may be brief, it is possible to discuss: why the referral was made, who is worried, what the worries are, what behaviours are causing concern and to whom, and (most importantly) agree on how much of what the adolescent tells me I may pass on. Sometimes, especially if it seems that I may end up offering the adolescent help directly, we may agree that everything said to me will be in confidence. In other circumstances we agree that I will talk to the social worker about my assessment, ideally with the adolescent present. It always surprises me how often teenagers agree to this arrangement and (more importantly) how often this arrangement seems to help. I know that the adolescent's agreement may be yet another sign of the pseudo-compliance of the distressed individual, from chaotic and abusive homes, who has been 'through the social services' system and knows it inside out. I also have no doubt that often a really confidential talk to an adult can be of great help to a teenager, but I also know that such individuals can be helped if some information is shared. I will return to this point later in this chapter.

Terry made it clear at the very start of our meeting that it was most certainly *not* his idea to see me. But I knew that, however reluctantly, he had agreed to see me 'just once'. I will very rarely agree to see an adolescent against their wishes, and indeed by this age most teenagers, unless locked up in secure accommodation, can very easily avoid meetings they wish to miss. And indeed, in my experience, many do!

How often has a social worker rung me to say, 'Sorry, Paul, Jenny's done a runner! She wasn't at home when I called for her this morning. Can you offer her another appointment?'

> So I make the assumption that perhaps a little bit of Terry does want to see me even if he proclaims otherwise.
>
> 'I don't know. But you did get here this morning. I'm sure that you could have found ways to avoid coming.'
>
> 'But Mary says she wants me to see you. But I'm not mad, you know. I don't need to see a shrink!'
>
> Terry's comments are my clue how to continue our meeting. I feel that progress is being made and that Terry has (albeit in an indirect and rather negative way) expressed one of his real concerns: madness. Certainly his father's madness and perhaps his own.
>
> So, not surprisingly, one of the core issues and tasks of the meeting, madness, has been named by Terry.

It is often this way, we all have a tendency to 'spill the beans' of what worries us however hard we may try to control what we say and disclose. When training as an individual psychotherapist I was taught that the first comments a patient makes during a session might form the basis of the content of the session, whatever other material is subsequently raised. Indeed it has been suggested that the *first* dream retold by the patient to the therapist in the first sessions of a treatment can (in symbolic terms) describe the core of the problem to be focused on for many months to come.

Marcia Karp (who trained me as a psychodramatist) teaches that in psychodrama the director (therapist) must listen very carefully to the protagonist's (patient's) first words, which form a sort of 'contract', defining the issues or problems on which they wish to work in that session.

And the same is sometimes true in initial or assessment interviews with adolescents. The problem is how to use one's hunches. To rush in too fast with a comment to Terry such as, 'perhaps you are very afraid of madness, yours and other people's,' may be very relevant to him but it might well result in his precipitous flight towards the door of my room! One could wait until the young person feels able or willing to talk more directly about his or her preoccupations or worries. However such a point may very well never be reached. The adolescent will, in powerful silence or small talk, wait, becoming ever more anxious. This increasing distress may too result in the premature termination of the meeting!

Under stress all of us tend to become anxious; however, as we develop as children and adolescents we develop tactics to cope with new or stressful situations. Such developments are signs of increasing psychological maturity. The distressed or disturbed adolescent, however, may not yet have made these advances (or in a crisis may lose what skills have been acquired). In an initial meeting with me they may regress to quite primitive, childlike, ways of feeling, with a sense of omnipotence or its opposite, complete helplessness in the face of the powerful 'other'. They may project their anger on to me, feeling as a result persecuted and attacked. Or their anxiety may increase to such a level that they begin to feel as if they are falling to pieces, their distress, anger and panic having no holding or containing boundaries. In such circumstances is it a surprise that an adolescent needs to terminate the interview and leave the room in a hurry?

Infants are often in such a state of unheld (or contained) panic and distress. It is their relationship with their mother (but of course not only the mother) which can calm them. The parent uses soothing words, physical holding, ideally in an environment where both the mother and infant feel safe. I believe that similar principles hold for the emotional holding of distressed children, adolescents and adults. Indeed I learnt, while consultant to a day assessment unit in Wandsworth, that really disturbed children often still need physical

11 'Why should I talk to you?'

holding, almost like an infant, when they are at their most distressed and panicky.

Josephine Klein (1987)[1] describes with great clarity how certain patients (often with appalling infancies and childhoods) react in psychotherapy (a process that may result in 'regression' in the consulting room) and how their therapists may best try to 'hold' them. Much of what she says about this (and other topics) is, in my opinion, highly relevant to interviews with adolescents. There is no space however in this chapter to discuss further the issues of the containment (or holding) of anxiety; I recommend that the interested reader looks at Josephine Klein's book. I believe that, if the adolescent is to be 'held' in the interview, a balance must be struck between a style that is too passive, in which one waits for the young person to start talking, and a manner which is too hasty or inquisitorial. The former may allow the adolescent's panic at the unknown (me! if I'm the interviewer) to rise too far, while the latter may only confirm the young person's opinion that they are just in the room to have uncomfortable facts and secrets dug out of them.

On the whole I take an active approach, believing that if I talk (and thus let the adolescent know a little more about me), I can help put them at ease. In my experience teenagers respond well to an adult who talks, who takes calculated risks in what he says, *and* listens to the answers.

But what can I say or ask?

Some of the possible questions seem obvious: 'How do you feel today?', a question which rarely gets an answer and may only increase anxiety; 'What's your problem?', also often a non-starter, as is, 'Why have you come to see me?'...'My social worker told me I had to come!'

'What do you like best at school?' was an old faithful question for the early stages of interviews, but these days not always a safe or sensible one to ask disturbed teenagers who may not have been to school for months or even years.

Friendly questions about the family (which may work well at the local scout group or church youth club) are also best avoided in the early stages of assessment meetings.

In my experience it is usually better to try to get a sense of where the adolescent is 'at'. Such questions can only be formulated if I try to think how I might feel in his position.

> 'You know Terry, you seem very tense to me, perhaps you are really angry at being brought to see a psychiatrist!'
> 'I'm not mad!'
> 'You know I see very few mad teenagers, most boys I see of your age are just unhappy, upset and a bit confused.'

Silence.
(It's too early in the session for me to be sure that Terry isn't mad. My early impression however is of his sanity.)
'Perhaps you really don't know if you can trust me. Why should you? This is the first time we've met.'

Some of my questions are made after I consider how I feel at the time in the room with the youngster.

I have a feeling of some tension and anxiety (not surprising in a first interview. I usually feel a little apprehension before meeting any new patients). I am also aware of feeling a little gloomy and downcast.
'I get the feeling that you might be feeling a little low and fed up this morning.'
'Wouldn't you?'
'I don't know. Do you know why you're a bit sad?'
'I miss my dad. He's in hospital again.'
'I know. your social worker told me.'
The interview is underway.

In order to help Terry I took a risk. He had not told me he felt sad, nor had his social worker who was more worried by serious 'madness' rather than ordinary 'sadness'.

'Counter-transference' is the term used in psychoanalytic theory to describe the feelings that occur in the therapist during a session with a patient (see Sandler, Dare and Holder, 1973, for a clear review of the development of this concept).[2] While talking to Terry I had a sense of sadness, tension and some anxiety. I had felt a little anxious before our meeting, but had not felt particularly downcast or gloomy. These feelings might originate from various sources. Put simply they include:
1. Feelings I have that day, totally unrelated to my assessment interview with Terry (e.g. worry or sadness about a recent disagreement with a close friend).
2. Feelings, the origins of which I'm aware, resulting from my meeting with this boy (e.g. my normal slight anxiety that occurs before any first interview). It is also very possible to experience quite rational feelings when in contact with another (e.g. anger at a client who arrives very late for a meeting or when someone is simply insulting). These feelings may however also indicate something more complex and important about the psychological workings of the other person (see 4 below).
3. Feelings that occur in me as the result of *my* 'transference' reaction to Terry. I respond to Terry as if he were an important

person from my past (a relationship that thus has become part of my 'inner world'. We all tend, at times, to react to others in ways more appropriate to people from our past (including our former selves!). Transference is discussed in more detail below.

4. Finally, the feelings I experience may be the result of Terry's relationship and transference *to me*. The ways in which his transference relationship to me 'manipulates' my feelings is subtle and complex. An awareness of how I feel might give me some information about what is going on (at a conscious and unconscious level) in the boy I'm talking to.

I am suggesting that we all stir up feelings (as well as thoughts) in each other in any interaction or relationship which are, in part, related to our 'inner worlds' with all their strengths, complexities and problems. It is thus possible to divide those feelings in me that result from my contact with Terry into those of 'neurotic counter-transference' originating from my past and problems, and those of 'therapeutic counter-transference' that can provide me with information about the young man sitting in front of me.

Heinrich Racker (1968)[3] suggests that the therapist identifies with aspects with the patient in two ways. There are 'concordant ego identifications' which are based on the recognition that what belongs to (and exists in) another person also belongs to one's own psychological self. We have all been adolescent and can recognise aspects of ourselves in our clients. This helps our understanding of them.

Racker also describes 'complementary identifications' in which the client projects one of his internal 'objects' (say his father) on to the professional, who then identifies with this projection and begins to feel like the client's father.

Both types of identification can aid the process of understanding another person. He stresses the point that patient and therapist are in a relationship, both reacting to each other, both producing thoughts and feelings in the other partly based on present reality, partly determined by the two 'inner worlds' that are meeting.

The task of the therapist or person interviewing a client is to be as aware as possible of their own internal psychological processes, for it is highly dangerous to attempt to attribute to the other person feelings that have their origins entirely in our own internal world — feelings that Racker attributes to the 'counter-transference neurosis' of the therapist.

Self-awareness is, in my opinion, a crucial requisite for those working (in any capacity) with disturbed individuals. Such self-knowledge can arise from an honest experience of life: it can also be increased by personal therapy or through good supervision in a work setting. Indeed this conscious and unconscious awareness of the other person's position and mental state is the foundation of all good human interactions, and empathy, the process that allows one person to feel for another.

I certainly don't tell the client that 'sitting here with you in this room makes me feel sad/angry/abused/mad!...And I assume that these feelings are highly relevant to how *you* feel!' No, the self-awareness must be used with tact and great caution. It is a 'trick of the trade'. If used with discretion it can greatly facilitate potentially difficult interviews, and I have discovered over the years that an active, but appropriate use of these phenomena can help a silent or sullen teenager feel understood.

'Perhaps it is really very difficult and painful to talk about these sad feelings about your dad.'

'They don't understand. Well my social worker does a bit, but...'

Terry once more lapses into silence.

I feel that by using the word 'understand' this sad boy is giving me the opening to talk more about his feelings. But I must be careful. I know that both his social worker and his foster parents are very experienced in work with troubled teenagers. I have no doubt that they have some understanding of this lad. I suspect that Terry has real fears of which might happen if he *talked*. Somehow action (however mad and destructive) may seem safer to him. I develop certain ideas, hypotheses about Terry's difficulties which I decide to test out in the interview.

'You know, we all get sad at times. But telling people about our feelings isn't always easy. you never know what they will do with them! Will they take them seriously? Will they use your talking about being sad to blame or attack you later? It's never easy talking!'

'And your dad?'

(I know I'm taking a risk now, linking his dad, who was once more in a psychotic breakdown, with feelings.)

'Oh, he's barmy, mad as a hatter! I get so pissed off with him!'

Progress. I decide to take another risk, since I feel that Terry is beginning to trust me a little.

'Perhaps when you feel upset or moody, with feelings like we all have at times, you wonder if you are going mad, like your dad. I mean you fear that you're going really mad!'

Silence. Terry shifts uneasily in his chair.

'Do you think I'm mad?'

'We've only just met, so I can't be really sure.'

11 'Why should I talk to you?'

(In my experience honesty always pays off, especially with adolescents.)
'But, so far, you seem pretty sane to me!'
Terry allows himself a slight smile, he relaxes a bit.
'However, your social worker tells me that you've been doing some rather odd things at your foster home.'
Terry doesn't like this comment, His smile fades and I feel his hackles rise and with them my anxiety, and (rather to my surprise) I begin to feel a sense of annoyance with this 'difficult boy'. I know I must now back pedal and proceed carefully if this interview is to continue. I feel a bit of a fool. I feel that I've blown it. I was warned that he didn't like people to talk about his 'odd' behaviour. But is this all? How else can I make sense of the present situation?

An objective look at my counter-transference reactions tells me several things:

As a professional I don't like making mistakes and I'm annoyed with myself for being rather too pushy with Terry and mis-timing my comment.

I know that I like to be held in good regard by social work colleagues. What will Mary think of me if Terry suddenly rushes down into the waiting room? Another failed interview! And no doubt there are other aspects of my personal (neurotic counter-transference) reaction to this situation.

But what can my feelings tell me about what is going on in Terry? He seems very anxious about his behaviour, worried that it means that he really is mad like his dad. Such worries are really often a sign of sanity. The start of self awareness and insight.

My sense of shame (and indeed almost humiliation) at having made a mess of the interview *might* relate to Terry's own feelings about the messes he makes of his life.

And 'might' is the operative word. Many (I guess most) of my feelings during an interview have nothing to do with the person opposite. The 'therapeutic counter-transference' must be used with care and caution.

And, I ask myself, who is Terry treating me like? What transference feelings and reactions are coming my way from this boy?

Ralph Greenson[4] defines transference as:

> The experience of feeling, drives, attitudes, fantasies and defences towards a person in the present which do not befit that person, but are a repetition of reactions originating in regard to significant persons of early childhood, unconsciously displaced onto figures in the present (Greenson 1967, P171).

Freud originally used the concept to describe the difficulties that occurred in a treatment when the patient reacted to his or her analyst as if they were 'someone else', usually someone from their past. As the years passed Freud, and his followers, began to see the transference as their 'best tool' in the treatment process. Psychoanalytic theorists differ as to whether the term *only* applies to the patients' relationships in the consulting room or can be observed in other situations.

Greenson writes:

> Transference occurs in analysis and outside of analysis in neurotics, psychotics, and in healthy people. All human relations contain a mixture of realistic and transference reactions (Greenson 1967, p.152).

I know something of Terry's background (having been given a social history by his social worker) and I begin to wonder *who* he is treating me as if I was. I am made to feel (in the countertransference) as if I've exposed and abused the boy. Humiliated him by just suggesting we talk about his bizarre behaviour in his foster home. I begin to wonder who else might have exposed, abused or humiliated this boy in his life. There are several obvious candidates including, of course, his parents and his mother's co-habitee.

How should I proceed?

I could ask Terry the direct question: 'Have you been abused? You get very upset and angry when people expose your behaviour or feelings. When they do this it seems to make you feel very small and humiliated.'

The very directness of these statements (especially if they seem appropriate to the adolescent) can lead to other problems. The correctness of relevance to the adolescent can terrify him: 'This guy's a mind reader! I never told anyone what happened to me.'

The comments to the adolescent must always be couched in a cautious way. Indeed I would very rarely interpret the nature of the adolescent's transference to me directly. He's not in psychotherapy with me, nor is the interview an assessment session for psychotherapy. I would however use my thoughts about the transference to help me think about the teenager and the way they react to the world. If they treat me in a certain way (in our first meeting) I might

11 'Why should I talk to you?'

expect that they would react to others in a similar way.

I now wonder if I can link two things I've learnt about young Terry; his strong sense that *no one* understands him and his rather negative response to my comments on his bizarre behaviour. I wonder who has, in the past made fun of his attempts to communicate about his feelings, who has teased about his behaviour. Was it his, at times drunken, mother? Was it his, at times mad, father? Was it his mother's violent cohabitee? I don't know, and it will be impossible for me to find out in this meeting, but these questions and thoughts help me with my next comment to Terry.

'You know, many people find it difficult to talk about feelings or worries, especially if in the past they have been teased or ignored when they have tried to tell other people.'

'Yes, my foster parents don't understand me. They're so different from my family.'

(I've been told that Terry's foster family are Pentecostal Christians, a caring but very different background to Terry's own natural family.)

'They want me to be just like their children. Well behaved, good at school. I'm not like that!'

I notice that Terry doesn't (can't) talk about his own parents where (I suspect) the problem started. No doubt talking or thinking about certain aspects of his own family is much too painful at present. I wonder however at the reality of the expectations of his foster parents. Although foster families in the 'teenage scheme' are not meant to 'claim' the teenagers placed in their families I've known many who do (for the very best of reasons) have expectations of the young people that are very different from their families of origin.

'You know, Terry. I wonder if the problem with communication is partly your problem and partly the problem of those around you. You really do feel very upset, confused and a bit sad, but find it very difficult to put these feelings into words. Other people, however, perhaps don't always listen to you or understand you.'

'But I'm not mad! Am I?'

The interview has now progressed and I've been talking to Terry for half an hour.

'No, you're not mad. And I'm an expert in madness! I'm trained and paid to see a few mad people. And as the expert I can tell you that you're OK!'

This is a regular line of mine in my clinic! It amazes me how often I'm asked to say if an adolescent is 'mad'. The turmoil of the disturbed teenager can be alarming, destructive, dangerous and at times bizarre, but usually (but of course not always) different from the real madness of adults. I often guess from talking to a social worker that the adolescent they are worried about is not 'mad'. However I have to do an assessment to convince both parties of the young person's (relative) sanity! And, of course, from time to time, I do meet a really disturbed adolescent.

I feel that much of my work with teenagers, and that of many others who struggle with difficult adolescents, involves giving the young person a language and a vocabulary to help them express and communicate their feelings. A child, adolescent, or for that matter an adult, without such skills must resort to other techniques, many of which may be destructive to self or others, (e.g. violence, crime, self abuse).

> Terry had been using rather bizarre and certainly destructive methods to communicate various feelings: sadness at the loss of his father to a psychiatric hospital, panic at his fears of his own madness, anger with his foster parents who wished him to be other than what he was, perhaps fear and resentment of his mother and her friend. And no doubt many other fears, frustrations and worries.
>
> There were several outcomes from my meetings (in the end I saw Terry twice). His social worker became less afraid of his 'madness' and more able to talk to Terry about 'sadness'. Terry was reassured of his sanity, and a bit better able to communicate with others.
>
> Eventually his foster placement broke down and (rather to Terry's relief I suspect) he moved into a children's home. I have often found that children from deeply traumatic and abusive families cannot cope (at least for some time) with the more ordinary, caring, parenting offered by foster parents. Such experiences stir up too much guilt and confusion.

In my years working with both adolescents and their social workers I have often noted that while the adult does understand the teenager's moods, worries and anxieties, they cannot express this understanding to their client. They may tell me 'I think Debby is really very sad that her dad has left home.' The professional *knows* much about the girl (through using her counter transference and empathy). But because Debby can't put her feelings into words, she doesn't say, 'I'm bloody mad with my dad,' or 'I'm really fed up today, I could kill myself!' No, she sulks, stays out all night with boys, or runs away from home. Are they risking violence or a suicide attempt if they put their hunches into words? Will the girl become more disturbed? The social worker feels very stuck. It is as if they fear to distress the adolescent more by showing that they understand. In my experience teenagers can be assisted when I am able to help the adults in their lives think about them. To do this I have to tell the professional something of what the adolescent has told me. However such information can *only* be shared with young people's permission. I believe that my discussions with the adults help to contain their feelings (often panicky) about their young clients. Only if they feel 'held' (by their supervisor, colleagues or through discussions with me) will they be able to help the adolescent. A distressed, depressed or panicky mother can rarely provide her infant with 'good enough' parenting.

In my experience I believe that the ability to *understand* an adolescent and to be able to *communicate* this understanding to the young person is often a very powerful and healing experience. But, when understood, the young person must also feel safe, contained, held emotionally. Their lives are often awful beyond belief. For an adult to say, 'I know, I have some understanding of what you've gone through, indeed what you're going through now,' and to want no more from the young person and not to use this understanding as the source of power for further abuse, may be a powerful and unique experience for the teenager.

> Terry refused further appointments with me after our two sessions.
>
> 'He said I'm not mad. Why should I see a psychiatrist?'
>
> He did well in his children's home and eighteen months after I last saw him, he had me invited to his care review. He was in work, reasonably happy. An ordinary young man. He wanted to show me that we were both right in our understanding.
>
> Terry was not mad, just very sad and angry.

Acknowledgements

I would like to thank the many young people and their families who have helped me over the years discover more about adolescence. I would also like to thank the many colleagues and friends who supported me during my years in Wandsworth.

References

1. Klein, Josephine (1987) *Our Need for Others and its Roots in Infancy*, Tavistock Publications.

2. Sandler, J., Dare, C., and Holder, A. (1973) *The Patient and the Analyst. The basis of the psychoanalytic process*, Maresfield Reprints, London (1979).
3. Racker, Heinrich (1968) *Transference and Countertransference* Maresfield Reprints, London (1982).
4. Greenson, Ralph (1967) *The Technique and Practice of Psychoanalysis*, The Hogarth Press.

12 Listening and learning: psychodramatic techniques with children

Anne Bannister

Communicating

The need to communicate is a basic human instinct. To deprive someone of this is the most acute torture. Recently I saw a play about Edith Bone, a naturalised Englishwoman kept in solitary confinement for seven years in a Hungarian jail because the authorities assumed that she was spying for the British. She was released at the time of the Hungarian uprising in 1956. She was a very highly educated woman who kept sane by communicating with her own past life, which had been a rich and interesting one. But even she was profoundly grateful for the humanity provided by one of her jailers. He was a simple man, uneducated, but he communicated with her on an emotional level and helped her through the isolation of part of that time. He listened with interest to her stories. By planting a sunflower seed in the prison yard where Edith could see it grow, he demonstrated that he understood her needs.

A child communicates with its mother through cries and smiles, through behaviour, and, very soon, through play. Children learn to speak in an amazingly short period because of their need to communicate. Mothers of large families often find that the youngest child is late in talking because older brothers and sisters provide for the child's needs without the use of words so the baby takes her time in learning to talk.

A baby needs to communicate not only in order to meet her practical needs; her emotional needs are equally important. Fashions in childcare have moved from Truby King's strict regime, through Dr Spock to Penelope Leach and at last we are beginning to understand the child's need to communicate her feelings. The next step is for those feelings to be given the same respect as those of an adult. Alice Miller (Miller, 1987)[1] calls this lack of respect 'the vicious circle of contempt'. We can see it in action in any children's playground. A child picks a beautiful golden flower and takes it to his mother, she looks at him indulgently. 'It's a dandelion,' she says. 'It's only a weed,' and she drops it carelessly on the ground. The dismayed child tries to hide his feelings and runs away across the playground to where a younger child is also picking dandelions to give to her mother. The older child grabs the flowers and dashes them to the ground. 'Don't be stupid,' he cries contemptuously. 'They're only weeds.' The little girls cries but no-one notices.

Both those children recognised beauty when they saw it but the adult told them that they were wrong. In order to gain power for ourselves we must show that we are more knowledgeable and that we know the rules. Power can be used to protect, to support and encourage so there is nothing intrinsically bad about it. So why do adults so often use it to demean children? Violet Oaklander (Oaklander, 1978),[2] who is a therapist working with children, says, 'Every time a child opened his or her heart to me and shared that amazing wisdom usually kept hidden away, I felt awe. The children I have worked with may not know it, but they have taught me much about myself.'

I think the key phrase here is 'that amazing wisdom usually kept hidden away'. Why do children not share this more easily? It may be because we do not listen. We cannot accept that years of work and learned study to produce a blue rose may not, in the end, create a flower that is more beautiful than the simple dandelion. We therapists spend hours digging patiently to find our client's true feelings, in order to facilitate healing. The young child has not buried his or her feelings so deeply and can share these more easily, if only we will listen. The child can then complete her own healing and, in the process, teach the therapist a great deal too.

Another reason why children do not share their knowledge is that they try to protect adults and also that children are egocentric and believe that they are the cause of events which concern them. A good example from literature is of Simon Gillayley, age 7, in Keri Hulme's book *The Bone People*.[3] Simon is being viciously beaten by his stepfather, Joe, who in other respects is kind and caring. Simon and

12 Listening and learning

his stepfather make friends with a woman, Kerewin, whom both respect. Joe feels that Simon will tell about the abuse. 'Have you told Kerewin?' Joe asks his stepson. Simon shakes his head. 'Why not?' asks Joe. 'Because she'll know I'm bad,' the child replies.

I am sometimes taken to task by parents and professionals because I prefer parents not to accompany their children to therapeutic or assessment sessions with me. If supportive parents bring their child along I prefer the parent to wait in a completely different part of the building, or to go out for a walk during the session. This is because children so often feel that abuse which they have suffered was done because they were bad, because they deserved it, and they are fearful of allowing the parent to see or hear this. They also are most protective of their parents, knowing that mother will be upset, father will be angry when they hear about the abuse the child has suffered. Children can judge this much better than I can. Usually, especially with older children, I videotape my therapeutic sessions, with the consent of parent and child. The tape is not shown to anyone until therapy has progressed somewhat. I then ask the child if the tape can be shown to a parent, who is receiving simultaneous work with another therapist or social worker.

One 12-year-old girl was now living with father and stepmother, having been removed from mother and stepfather: the latter had sexually abused her. The girl's stepmother was supportive and understanding but dad was finding it difficult to cope. The girl had developed a flirtatious manner with men as a result of the abuse. It was a common coping mechanism which helped her to deny that the experience was abusive. Father could not understand this and was afraid of it. There was a family row when he hinted that it must have been her own fault that she was sexually abused.

At the next session the child asked if her father and stepmother could see the videotaped sessions we had had early on in therapy. With me she revealed herself as a deeply depressed little girl. There was no trace of the flirtatious young woman. She told me how she had looked after her younger siblings when her father left her mother with three young children under five. She had also supported her mother who struggled with her own deep depression for several years. She had greeted the arrival of a stepfather with relief, as someone to share the burden and, of course, she trusted him completely as she tried to be friendly to him so that he would stay and help them all. She had demonstrated all her feelings to me in the sessions by body posture and by role play, so her father was perhaps not prepared for the impact of the video when he saw it. His wife said she had never seen him cry before. At last he understood. The parents' social worker reported a great improvement in family relationships and the girl began to build her confidence again. She had known what to do and when to do it. I acted only as her facilitator.

This little girl, like Simon Gillayley in fiction, felt that she was bad so the abuse must have been her fault. She even tried to prove it to herself by acting flirtatiously when men were around. After being able to express her deepest feelings to someone who listened she began to understand what she must have always known, that she did not deserve to be abused. When she was ready, and when she judged her father to be ready, she asked me to help. She needed to tell her father how it had been for her during the past seven years since he left, but she was not sure that he would listen. Watching the videotape in my office, he had to listen, and he understood.

Jacqueline Spring, the author of *Cry Hard & Swim: the story of an incest survivor*,[4] describes beautifully how the therapeutic process mirrored her relationship with her own mother. Jacqueline is describing her work with 'Eve' her therapist.

> I was filled with exactly the feelings I would have experienced upon trying to tell my mother at the time it actually happened. Split many ways, I wanted to be protected from Eve's horror, shock, anger, disgust, withdrawal. With another part of me I wanted to protect Eve from the impact of what I was saying, to minimise. And yet I also wanted, silently cried out for her to protect me. I would have given anything in the world just to be taken in her arms and cuddled...Most extreme of all was the fear of her disbelief. On the child level I was sure she would not be able to accept this torrential pain I was pouring out, any more than my mother could have, that she would downplay everything and accuse me of overdramatising.

Listening

What Jacqueline Spring was expressing was the child's wisdom in knowing that her mother could not have borne the pain if she had told her at the time. She was afraid that no-one could bear it but Eve had obviously convinced her that she would listen and that she could bear the pain. Therapeutic listening is extremely powerful. In an article in *The Observer* (July 1989) an anonymous woman talks about her experience of attending a Brook Clinic for help after an abortion. The woman, now a therapist, said, 'To be listened to, to be understood, not to be judged — this is where true healing lies.'

Therapy with adults can take months and years. To be listened to, at last, after a lifetime of being ignored, is a long and slow process. I am often amazed at how quickly some children respond to a therapeutic listening session. Obviously it depends on how often the child has been misunderstood, disbelieved or contemptuously discounted. It depends also on how often someone has tried to listen and support. This is always part of my assessment of the child. To find the child's ally or supporter is not only helpful from a practical point of view but it also is helpful in assessing the extent of damage done to the child. A good ally, who can also be supported professionally, can do much to continue the work with the child after the therapy has officially ceased. On the other hand, the lack of any allies at all is a signal that the child will need more long-term work to re-establish belief in herself as a person to be respected and someone worthy of supporting. Some children have had no opportunity to practise the role of being protected or supported. They were always protecting others and supporting them. Such children are extremely vulnerable to further abuse and part of the therapy will be to practise being a child, to be listened to, to play, to be cared for.

Many children find it strange to be confronted by an adult whose only agenda is to listen to them. They seek the hidden agenda. Maybe this woman is a teacher trying to get me to learn something? Maybe she's like my mother trying to get me to love her? Or perhaps she's like my aunt and uncle who want to play rude games with me? They test me out, seeking the boundaries, seeking clues to my behaviour. To help them, and me, I set the boundaries for the session clearly at the beginning.

I try to ensure that the child is carefully prepared for a session with me by a parent or professional. We talk about the explanations to be given to the child and the reasons for attending. Then I repeat those explanations directly to the child, age appropriately, of course. Sometimes I have to repeat those reasons for more than one session. Then the child and I negotiate boundaries of time and space for the session, and also boundaries of behaviour are established fairly early on. Whilst setting these boundaries I make it clear that I will take responsibility for them. I may encourage a child to hit and kick and scream but if so I take responsibility for seeing that he does not hurt himself or me or damage the room.

These issues of boundaries and responsibility are, of course closely linked with the issue of control, which will be a key factor in any session with an abused child. Virginia Axline (Axline, 1969)[5] comments, 'A child needs a certain amount of control. He is not entirely self-sufficient. The control that is the outgrowth of mutual respect seems to be far more conducive of good mental attitudes than any other method of control.' She points out that in therapy the child is given the opportunity to get rid of his tensions and in so doing to gain an understanding of himself that enables him to control himself. I would add that not only does he rid himself of his tensions but he is able to express all his feelings, if listened to, and understood. Thus may he understand himself and provide his own controls.

In psychodrama we have a method of allowing a person to listen to herself as a child. We ask the protagonist, or client, to become herself as a child, which she may do in stages during a long session. When she is truly able to feel again those feelings she had as a child she is asked to re-create a scene when she tried to express those feelings but was not heard. There is often a painful re-enactment of an abusive situation or sometimes a situation which appears to be quite ordinary; a situation where the child's feelings were simply ignored or misunderstood. In Alice Miller's terms this mistreatment certainly felt abusive to the child, and of course it is the child's perception that we are dealing with. We ask the protagonist to reverse roles with the parent or significant other so that she can see herself through the other's eyes and perhaps gain some understanding of the other's point of view. Sometimes we ask another group member to stand in for the 'child' so the protagonist can see herself projected on the psychodramatic stage but she can be distanced from it. This is known as the 'mirror' technique and helps the protagonist to find a solution to the problem because only she knows the answer. The depth of feeling may be clouding her judgement so looking through the 'mirror' makes it more clear. Sometimes we have to provide an 'ideal mother or father'. The protagonist chooses someone from the group who can play her ideal parent. This is always someone who will listen and be with the child. The director asks the protagonist to role reverse and become the ideal parent to ensure that the person playing the role knows what is needed. Then the client reverses to playing herself as a child with the ideal parent listening carefully and sharing her experiences. This technique has provided the opportunity for hundreds of troubled adults to replay a part of their childhood to ensure that someone listened. There are many testaments to the efficacy of this therapy.

Perhaps it is not surprising that psychodrama can be so successful. When Jacob L. Moreno developed the method, in the 1920s, he was seeking to harness that which was already there, in the child and in the therapist. He provided a facilitating method to allow people to listen to themselves and to be listened to in an active way. Our listening must be active, we must show that we have heard. When I am working with children I often simply repeat what the child is saying. I do this so that the child knows she is heard. I might then listen carefully for the statements she is making in body language and symbolism and try to repeat some of these for the child to hear. It is important, though, not to be too interpretive or 'clever'. If I make a mistake the child will usually correct me, if respect has been sufficiently established so that she knows it is safe to do so. If I am completely wrong the child will ignore me and we will have taken a step backwards in the therapeutic process because she will feel that I was not listening.

Learning

Using psychodramatic techniques with children is often easier than with adults because it is simply repeating what they do naturally anyway. Children frequently reverse roles, 'You be me and I'll be the teacher.' They frequently use the 'mirror' technique showing with puppets or dolls what is happening to 'the little girl or boy'. They often use an ideal parent: 'You be my mum and I'll be your baby.'

Frank was a little seven-year-old boy who had been brought up in a loving but rather repressive household. Sexual matters were never mentioned and he was very aware, because his father had impressed it upon him, of his masculine role in protecting his mother from unpleasant happenings. Consequently when he was caught up in a child sex ring along with other boys he was unable to tell either parent. He thought that his mother could not listen because she would be shocked and hurt and his father could not listen because he would be angry. In fact his assessment was entirely correct. When the ring was discovered, through another child, Frank became depressed and withdrawn and failed to show any interest in school or friends, and his mother complained that she could not reach him.

Frank moved slowly with me at first, trying to discover whether I would react to his story angrily or with shock and horror. There was a long period of reassurance where we talked about familiar things and played dramatic games with puppets. He tested me out by picking up a boy doll. 'This boy is naughty, he takes his clothes off.' We explored the statement. When was it OK to take your clothes off and when was it not OK? 'What if a man tells him to take his clothes off?' he asked. We agreed that the boy doll couldn't help it if the man was big. He played the role of the man for a few moments, relishing the power and control that gave him. Without any direction he moved into the 'mirror technique' and picked up a puppet that he said was the monster man. He asked me to make the monster frighten the little boy doll. He watched intently while I demonstrated. I did not, of course, show specific abuse because he had not revealed this to me at this stage but I showed the usual sort of scary monster that appears in children's stories. 'He likes being scared,' he said calmly, giving me a clue that part of Frank's problem may be about coping with the pleasure as well as the pain of abuse.

Later on in therapy he was able to use the 'mirror' technique again, this time using anatomically correct dolls which he controlled himself to show me exactly what happened. 'I liked it a little bit and I was scared as well,' he said. He was able to express all his feelings, not just those he thought I wanted to hear. After three sessions Frank's mother reported a great improvement and his teacher was delighted that Frank was again showing interest in schoolwork. Of course his mother received parallel work from another worker to help her cope in the future.

Another psychodramatic technique is that of the 'multiple self'. It is used to clarify feelings for the protagonist. Roy was a ten-year-old who was sexually abusing younger children and even the pets kept at the children's home in which he was living. He had a long history of physical and emotional abuse and neglect by his parents and of sexual abuse by other relatives. He saw himself as wholly bad. He set out nursery chairs to represent some of the bad bits of himself and also the good bits. He sat on each chair in turn and I listened as he told me how he felt when he was stealing, for instance, or when he was being helpful to staff in the home. His 'good bits' asked questions of his 'bad bits' and vice versa. It emerged that he was quite unable to see what was wrong with abusing others. The only consequences that he could see were that he might get caught or that God would be cross with him.

Roy's favourite 'chair' in the multiple self game was that of 'baby'. He thoroughly enjoyed being a baby, sucking a baby bottle, being tucked up in bed and so on. He frequently returned to this role throughout the sessions, reminding me that he was just trying out his 'baby' chair. It seemed possible that Roy had never been allowed to be a baby and so he relished the opportunity within the sessions. I tried to use this later on to help him to gain empathy with his victims. By helping him to realise that his 'baby' had been a victim I hoped he could identify more with those he victimised. He resisted this firmly, saying the baby didn't care and that nothing hurt the baby. I realised this was Roy's only defence but also knew that what had been an appropriate defence mechanism for many years was now totally counter-productive and was preventing him from functioning and interacting with peers and adults. It was a very dangerous situation, especially as Roy grew bigger and stronger and, therefore, more of a threat to others.

In an early session he said there were two things he did not want to talk about. One was an incident when he had been accused of setting fire to a house in which he was living and the other subject not to be mentioned was one to which he would not even give a name.

As he was telling me about these two 'unspeakable subjects' he picked up some rolled up newspapers which I keep as a 'hitting stick' in the therapy room. He started to hit a large red bean bag and

12 Listening and learning

I suggested this might be a fire. He hit it harder and harder, releasing pent up anger and frustration. Eventually he said the fire had gone out. Later he was able to tell me the truth about the fire incident and to lay it to rest. His second unspeakable subject he eventually named as 'rude things'. He built a tower of red bean bags and picked up his hitting stick and started to knock it down. Suddenly in the middle of this he turned completely around. A number of rag dolls were sitting on two chairs behind him. 'I'm killing all the mums and dads,' he shouted, and knocked them violently onto the floor, beating them again and again with heartfelt fury. It was not important, from a therapeutic point of view, to question his connection of 'rude things' and his parents. It was enough that I had listened and he had expressed his anger. Of course if Roy had been living with his parents I might have felt it necessary to explore the connection as soon as possible.

However, Roy remained a very difficult child to reach. In one session he spent most of the time symbolically destroying all the dolls in the room after naming them as mums and dads, grandparents, aunts and uncles, and brothers and sisters. Only the baby was left and he beat that repeatedly with the hitting stick. 'He's not dead,' he said, 'but he's covered in bruises.' I tried to introduce an ally, someone who would listen. I used an angel puppet. Roy killed that too. I tried a cuddly bear puppet with big ears 'for listening with'. Roy sat dejectedly in the middle of the therapy room while the puppet stroked his hair. I told him the bear could tell how he was feeling. For the first time in our sessions he showed his vulnerability as the bear comforted him, 'listening' to his pain. Roy still has a long way to go before his bruises will heal.

Another technique of psychodrama which can be used to facilitate a child is that of the 'double'. A 'double' is someone who plays the inner self of the protagonist. A double speaks the words which the protagonist finds hard to say. A double must have empathy for the protagonist and it must be understood that the protagonist can challenge the double and correct what is being said. Doubles are used frequently in psychodramas with adults who have spent years repressing their feelings, especially about one particular person. With children the use of the double can often be a single intervention which encourages the child to express true feelings. Working on a one-to-one basis with a child I often start a role-play with myself as a significant other (often a parent) and, using role reversal, establish a scene where the child is actually telling the parent how she feels. If I sense that she is still protecting the parent I use a doll or simply an empty chair for the parent (depending on the age of the child) and become the child's 'double', speaking the words she really wishes to say. Of course a good deal of trust must have been established by this time so that the child can contradict me if I get it wrong, and in contradicting me she can affirm her true feelings. The 'double' is also acting as a role model here to show a child that it is acceptable to express feelings even to an adult upon whom one relies for protection.

Sometimes a 'double' merely supports the child in action. Karen was eight and was struggling to regain her sense of self-worth after sexual abuse by her grandfather. In role play she showed me that he had frequently assured her that the abuse was all right and that she liked it really. In psychodrama she started to tell him that she didn't like what he did. As her 'double' I repeated what she had often told me, that it hurt and it felt bad. Thus encouraged she launched into a very strong tirade against her grandfather, telling him that what he was doing was 'wrong' and that he was 'bad' to do it and that he should not make her feel bad. Afterwards she seemed to grow an inch or two as she realised that her feelings had been right all along and it was her grandfather who had 'got it wrong'. To make her grandfather listen to her, even in role-play, was immensely therapeutic for Karen and she seemed to recover quite quickly, with the help of her mother who was encouraged to boost Karen's self esteem as much as possible in the ensuing months.

The inner voice

Listening to children also encompasses listening to the voice of our own inner child. In Alice Miller's book *For your own good: the roots of violence in child rearing*[6] she states: 'The greatest cruelty that can be inflicted on children is to refuse to let them express their anger and suffering except at the risk of losing their parents' love and affection. The anger stemming from early childhood is stored up in the unconscious and since it basically represents a healthy, vital source of energy, an equal amount of energy must be expended in order to repress it...' In other words, if we are not listened to as a child our childhood spirit will not flourish and the energy that should have been expended in nourishing it will be used to repress it.

One such person was Sylvia. I was introduced to her when I worked in a centre where parents came to learn parenting skills in an effort to keep families together. Sylvia was 35 years old and when I met her she was a single parent with a new baby. She had been known to various official agencies for about fourteen years, since her first child was born illegitimately. She usually presented as an attractive young woman, well spoken, but with difficulties in reading and writing. The story she told was a sad one. She was brought up in a northern town with middle-class parents who ran a small business. She and her sister went to local schools where her sister apparently

12 Listening and learning

did well, eventually becoming a nurse. Sylvia told us she did not do so well at school but that, she said, was because she was 'thick'. She told us that she met a boy at fifteen and became pregnant. Her parents were shocked and horrified so she left home to live briefly with the boyfriend who, in turn, abandoned her when the baby was a few months old. During the next fifteen years she had seven children, with different fathers, and she physically abused or neglected them all, in turn, so that they had all been removed into the care of the Local Authority. None of the fathers had supported her and now she was attending the Centre in an effort to keep Julie, her new baby, with her.

Sylvia's social worker could not hide her relief as she handed over a neat file containing a precis of Sylvia's history. Unusually she did not want to discuss Sylvia with me, she had an urgent appointment, it was all in the notes, she wished me the best of luck. I had met Sylvia once, at an introductory meeting with the social worker but this had not prepared me for the information in those notes. Sylvia was feared by her social worker, her doctor, the local Social Security Office, even the police. I tried to remember what she looked like. I remembered a slightly built, rather pale young woman. Were we talking about the same person? Apparently, if Sylvia did not get her own way she threw a tantrum. She had pushed a filing cabinet over on to her social worker and thrown a brick through the glass panel in the Social Security Office. She had been charged with obstructing the police and been removed from so many doctors' lists that at present no general practitioner would accept her. The local casualty department was also getting rather tired of her presence. There had been one or two doubtful incidents in her past when a house had gone up in flames and a boyfriend had suffered stab wounds but, since the boyfriends were often wanted by the police, these incidents had never been fully explained. Many professionals had tried hard to help Sylvia. Naturally dependence on alcohol or drugs had been suspected, but nothing was proved and Sylvia always denied taking anything stronger than her favourite cigarettes. She had been seen by a psychiatrist and a psychologist but 'personality disturbance' was the best diagnosis that could be given. Her last social worker was convinced that the truth lay with Sylvia's parents and had asked her if they were still alive. Sylvia said that they were. She had not seen them for years. They had retired to a seaside town where she had never visited them but she knew their address through her sister, whom she occasionally telephoned.

The social worker visited the parents in their retirement bungalow. They seemed nice, middle-class, intelligent people who talked about Sylvia with sorrow rather than anger. Their story tallied with Sylvia's. Nothing in her childhood gave any clues to her present behaviour. The social worker telephoned Sylvia's sister and asked for an appointment, but she was a very busy nurse and could not spare the time. She thought that Sylvia must have some brain damage that caused her to behave as she did. The social worker knew that tests on Sylvia's brain had actually been carried out, with negative results.

Sylvia's children had not been severely physically damaged. In fact only two of them had bruises and scratches but there had been many instances of neglect and those who had seen her rages were fearful for the children's safety. I talked to Sylvia with some trepidation. If I were responsible for removing her seventh child how would she react? I asked her if she would like to join a group of mothers where I was using psychodrama and dramatherapy as a method. She was happy to do so and she fitted into the group quite easily. The other mothers liked her and I learned not to use any exercises where the participants had to write because Sylvia would refuse to join in.

After some weeks, as trust grew in the group, several mothers worked on problems in a psychodramatic way, looking at current and past relationships and gaining strength from other women in the group. One day we did an exercise in 'guided fantasy'. The mothers were relaxed and asked to imagine a journey into their childhood, to recover some of those lost feelings and to get in touch with their inner child. They then drew a representation of their feelings and shared these drawings in the group.

Sylvia had drawn a door. She said she could not pass through it into her childhood. She looked small and vulnerable. The group offered to support her if she would make the journey through psychodrama. She nodded and clung to my hand. Then she curled up into a ball and began to sob helplessly, quietly. She was in her cot, in a dark room. She was alone. Slowly, painfully, Sylvia re-enacted scenes from her childhood. There were scenes where her father would become unreasonably angry over a small misdemeanour and beat her. Once he broke her arm and she and her mother carefully rehearsed the story they would tell at the hospital about how she had fallen. Sometimes she would be locked in her room for hours with her mother sometimes smuggling food in to her. All of the punishments were justified by both parents because she had been naughty. Sylvia's distress was focused on the fact that no-one had recognised her pain. Her parents and sister all confirmed that she was bad or stupid and she had accepted this without anger. No-one else knew of the situation and since her family were so respected in the community there was no likelihood of anyone believing Sylvia.

She had been encouraged to be grateful to her parents because

12 Listening and learning

they spent time and money on her. As a businessman her father was better off than many of her schoolfriends' parents so she was conscious daily of her privileged position. Later, in her twenties, she had tried to talk to her sister about what had happened, in an effort to put it into perspective. She wondered if her sister had the same experience? But her sister denied that there had been anything untoward in the family. It may be that the sister was treated differently, or perhaps she had someone outside the family in whom to confide. We cannot know. She must, however, have had some knowledge of what had happened to Sylvia but perhaps she too had repressed it and remembered only the pleasant aspects.

Sylvia had tried hard to forget and had almost succeeded. Only when her body re-experienced the pain and isolation as she curled up as a baby in her cot. was she able to remember what had been done to her. At last Sylvia's hurt child had someone who would listen. Sylvia as an adult and the other group members listened with all their senses. Some mothers shared their own abusive experiences in childhood or more recently occasions when they had been ignored and treated without respect by partners or by those in authority. Sylvia was helped by this sharing and over the ensuing weeks she began to express herself more appropriately. She found she could be angry without the group withdrawing their support. She learned to be assertive without being angry. She learned to cry, something she had seldom done before the psychodrama. She worked hard on building her relationship with her baby. Some months later, after she had left the Centre, she brought baby Julie to see me. The child was walking and talking and was, in all respects, a well-cared for and happy child. We looked at photographs of the baby and then awkwardly, she thrust a sheaf of papers into my hand. They were poems, dozens of them full of joy and pain. 'I went to the literacy class,' she explained. 'I felt a fool but it wasn't as bad as I'd expected. I wrote these myself.'

I have no doubt that Sylvia will continue to suffer deeply as she grieves for the loss of her own childhood and the loss of six of her children. She had anaesthetised herself from that pain in order to survive. She may always need much support from friends since her own inner resources are so fragile. But by listening to herself she helped her friends to listen. Her own inner child knew what she needed and her friends were able to take their cue from her. Learning from children is not culturally acceptable in our society. We learn from those with age and wisdom, or from those who have studied a subject for years, but children are often seen as a tabula rasa or blank slate waiting to be filled in. Surely learning is a two-way process. As the teacher shows the child how to complete a mathematical problem she can learn from the child what he needs to help him remember. Is it easier for this child if he is given plastic blocks to represent the numbers or does it help if more familiar objects such as food or toys are used to explain the concept of number? Each child may have a different answer but each child can teach us something.

Awareness

Recently at a conference for psychotherapists we were discussing the point that a therapist cannot take a client beyond the point where the therapist stands. In other words the therapist must have moved along her own continuum of self awareness at least to a point that is further than that of the client. This contention raises many questions about the training and personal exploration completed by psychotherapists before they begin to practise. It also emphasises the need for ongoing self exploration and support to be given to the therapist to enable growth to continue.

Many of us spend time and trouble making sure we have adequate supervision and support. We need an objective consultant who can tell us about the transference that may be happening between us and our client and who can flag up a warning when our own inner defences and prejudices colour our view of what is happening to the client. Talking about experiences, either with client groups or with individuals, to a skilled consultant is invaluable and is stressed in the training of most people in the arts and creative therapies as well as in more orthodox training such as that of a psychoanalyst.

However, such support is not always easy to find and sometimes sessions with a consultant can be few and far between. Working with children over the past fifteen years I have become conscious of how much I have learned about myself from them. In one child I would see reflected my own sibling jealousies. Through another I would get in touch with my own early resentments and fears. Children would bring me gifts of understanding into their own behaviour as well. Quite often I see children who have been 'programmed' not to reveal anything to me. Sometimes, if they are very small they kick and scream and express their anger and frustration against me since it has nowhere else to go. Older children repeat their 'programming' mechanically, holding their bodies stiffly, staring at their feet, and not allowing one small drop of feeling to spill into the room. Others are more graphic. One boy sealed his mouth with sticky tape, another whispered so softly it was impossible to hear. A three year old stuck tape over the mouths of all the dolls in the room. How can we help such children? We cannot tear off the tape. That would be a violation in itself. If we are allowed to do so perhaps we can demonstrate our willingness to listen, actively, and to learn from the child. Then, gradually, the child may learn to remove the tape herself.

Surely to deny a child self-expression in this way is the cruellest abuse of all? Of course physical and sexual abuse can cause obvious and lasting damage, but we know from research (Gelinas, 1983)[7] that this can be alleviated if the child finds an ally to share the experience. The ally must be able to support the child sufficiently to allow full expression of the child's feelings about the abuse. The majority of children are not physically or sexually abused, as far as we know, but how many have metaphorical sticky tape wrapped around them from the cradle? How many are dissuaded from expressing fear, anger, pain, laughter or joy because these emotions do not accord with the feelings of their parents or carers?

Many childcare workers will be familiar with the child who does not know how to play. Three-year-old Jenny was one such who attended our Centre for some months. She was always clean and beautifully dressed. She was well fed and as far as we knew had not been physically or sexually abused. She was attending the Centre with her mother, who was suffering from severe depression and had expressed fears that she might harm the child. Jenny stood at the edge of the playroom looking rather apprehensively at the other children and staff. She was horrified by the suggestion that she might join in a noisy game of Ring-a-Roses.

Her disdain and contempt for the sandtray was almost comic. The sight of other children finger painting produced such an aversive reaction that she wet herself, much to her own distress and embarrassment. All Jenny wanted to do was to sit down quietly and look at a book. She was allowed to do this for as long as she needed to. Staff gradually moved near to her and looked at the pictures with her. She enjoyed the quiet storytime after lunch. Her mother ignored her for long periods but flitted into the playroom occasionally to smile approvingly at Jenny and remind her to be a good girl.

Gradually Jenny's mother worked on her own lost childhood, through individual and group work, with her social worker and therapist. Slowly Jenny put her book down and spent time in the Wendy House, being the mother and admonishing the other children to keep clean and be good. Mealtimes were a trial to Jenny, who hated to see the mess produced by other children, and she asked politely for help if there was an item of food which she thought she might spill.

One day Jenny arrived at the centre wearing loose trousers and a top, like most other children. It had a picture of a rabbit on the chest. Usually she was wearing pastel coloured, neatly ironed dresses and cardigans. She was proud of her little tracksuit and must have felt more comfortable because she started to join in with 'Ring-a-Roses' and 'Hide-and-Seek'. Her mother was feeling better, her dependence on anti-depressants had been recognised and addressed and she was fighting the battle to become independent of them. She came more often into the playroom and watched happily whilst Jenny played with dolls or the dolls' house.

One afternoon all the children donned their plastic aprons ready for a messy time with paint. To the staff's surprise Jenny asked for an apron. She sat down and watched carefully whilst the others dug their fingers in the paint and smeared it happily over the paper. She began to enjoy it, mixing the colours to produce a glorious swirly pattern. She demanded more paper, different colours. She was so absorbed that she failed to notice when her mother came into the room and stood behind her. The staff were apprehensive but decided to wait for a reaction. Mother made no comment but just watched quietly. Suddenly Jenny realised she was not alone and she looked up. For a moment her eyes registered alarm, her body became rigid and she looked mutely at her mother. 'Can I play at that?' asked her mother. Jenny moved over and allowed her mother to join her. They were very proud of the picture they created together.

When society began to be more aware of sexual abuse, in the 1980s in Britain, we began to realise how we had been blaming the victim. Parallels were drawn with women who were raped and women who were physically abused by their husbands. All had been blamed for their own abuse. On a global scale whole races such as Australian Aboriginals were blamed for their own near-extinction. Gradually we are beginning to realise what has been done in the name of progress, which has sometimes been another name for the abuse of power. By listening to a single child we plant a sunflower seed. The long term effects could be truly magnificent.

(The names of all children and adults in this paper have been changed. Other personal details have also been changed to protect anonymity.)

References

1. Miller, A. (1987) *The Drama of being a Child* Virago Press Ltd.
2. Oaklander, Violet (1978) *Windows to our Children*, Real People Press, Moab, Utah.
3. Hulme, Keri (1985) *The Bone People*, Spiral and Hodder and Stoughton.
4. Spring, Jacqueline (1987) *Cry Hard and Swim: the story of an Incest Survivor*, Virago Press Ltd.
5. Axline, Virginia (1969) *Play Therapy*, Ballantine Books, New York.
6. Miller, Alice (1987) *For your own good: the roots of violence in childrearing*, Virago Press Ltd.
7. Gelinas, Denise (1983) 'The Persisting Negative Effects of Incest', *Psychiatry*, Vol. 46 (November, 1983).

Part 5
The way forward

13 Towards a child-friendly society

Penelope Leach

We all want to live and work in a more child-friendly society and feel that, whatever our starting point, things are getting better for children. Professionals working in health or education would like to be able to concern themselves more with the positive enhancement of children's development and less with compensating children for earlier disadvantage. Work in the social and legal fields would carry more satisfaction if it could strive to improve on the tolerable as often as it strives to protect from the intolerable. At present, though, we want in vain. Child protection and associated professions are struggling against a strengthening undertow of horror as more, and more institutionalised, child abuse is revealed. And as fast as professionals construct rafts to float their particular charges safely above it, they see them swamped when they themselves move on, administrative arrangements alter and financial constraints tighten. While innovative work by professionals can change individual lives in the here and now and signpost routes for policy-makers, only parents, on whom chldren's ongoing daily lives depend, can keep children permanently afloat and insist on the social and economic backing they need to do so. If we want to change this inimical society into a better place for all children, we have to do it with and through their parents.

Making a place for parenting

Many people believe that parenting — or, more accurately,

13 Towards a child-friendly society

mothering — was easier and more satisfactory in some unspecified part of the past. Whether that is true, or part of the universal tendency to see greener grass on the far side of fences, it is irrelevant. Societies do not run backwards. The more nostalgically we look back, the less creatively we can look forward. If we want to create a society in which people feel good about being parents, we have to find ways of doing it within the context of today.

Adult working lives are longer and more broken up than they have ever been before. Few people spend their working lives within one firm, climbing a single ladder of advancement from apprenticeship at 16 to retirement at 65. Almost everyone has to train, re-train and re-deploy to follow the shifting demands of developing technology and changing markets. That working pattern could comfortably encompass an open option to spend five years giving children a good start. Some people who elected to have children would choose to combine their early care with a training period, with the slower pace of part-time work or with a new venture in self-employment. But whether or not parents chose to undertake other work simultaneously, parenting would be recognised as their immediate priority and the most socially desirable job they could do.

As soon as rearing children had equal status with other kinds of work, information, education and vocational training for parenthood would obviously be made available to every schoolchild, just as they are available for other career options. Since children are especially interested in child development during the years when they are young enough to remember themselves as infants yet old enough to observe their parents parenting, education for parenthood should begin in infant schools. At school, at home and outside both, children, and especially adolescents, should see the parenting option seriously treated as a valuable investment in society's future. The more they are aware of priority being given to meeting *their* needs, the more likely they are to grow up assuming that their own children's needs should have priority.

Once a couple decided to have children, at whatever stage in their adult lives, they would be expected — and helped — to make each child the principal factor in their lifestyle decisions for at least two years, and a major factor forever. Instead of leaving children off job or housing applications for fear of being passed over for somebody childless, people would put those children in because their very existence brought the status and privileges necessary to their care. It sounds strange because we are accustomed to thinking about parenting (if we think about it at all) as an extra to be fitted around already full lives; a universal hobby that is inconvenient because it cannot be shelved during the working week. But if parenthood was thoughtfully and positively chosen by some people rather than taken for granted by almost all, those attitudes would change. There is a precedent for this different approach. Consider prospective adoptive parents. They do not expect, and their counsellors will not accept, a casual approach to taking a baby into the family. Having consciously wanted and waited for a child, those prospective parents have at least tried to think through a child's emotional importance and practical impact in their lives and see nothing inappropriate in advance discussion of a child's needs or their plans to fulfil them.

Parent-friendly professionals

Once a given couple had produced a child, we should accept that they are almost always the best people to care for him or her, not least because they are the people to whom the child will be most attached. If more of society's resources were used to help those in difficulty within their parenting, fewer would need to be used to help them out. Every time we arrange a nursery place for the child of a lone mother who is clinging to a safety net by her fingertips, we imply that her personal mothering is relatively unimportant; if she cannot cope with daily life with the child on whatever benefits she can claim, that child will be better off cared for by 'professionals' while she earns money. Every time a child is added to a Child Protection Register (let alone removed to 'a place of safety') the mother feels she is being told that her relationship with that child is worthless, her kind of parenting dangerous. As we reduce that mother's already crumbling self-esteem so we increase the likelihood of that prophecy becoming self-fulfilling. Of course there will always be children who, by the standards of the day, are neglected or physically, sexually or emotionally abused. But the more parent-friendly society becomes, the easier it will be for most parents to be child-friendly, so we could reasonably expect fewer tragedies. After all, while parents who hide children with epileptic disorders away in attics still exist, ridding those disorders of their shameful or devil-ridden connotations and offering medical and social help, has reduced what used to be common practice to a rare horror. We have everything to gain from strenuous attempts to keep families functioning happily because satisfactory alternatives are rare. When family care fails a child, being 'in care' often fails him too.

If parents — especially mothers — are not to be demeaned by social or economic pressures to pass their babies to professionals while they earn outside money, a variable period within home-base for each child has not only to be financed but also integrated into a supportive and companionable network for the parent(s). There are individuals who still choose, and manage to arrange, to live in extended families and/or communities where the care of the youngest members can be shared. But for most people today, being at home full-time is isolating and lonely and being constantly confronted with trivial and repetitive chores leads to an uncomfortable combination of overwork and boredom. The pressure for daycare from infancy probably arises as much from these negative aspects of 'staying at home' as from the positive aspects of working outside it.

A new look at daycare dilemmas

Society faces a decline in the pool of school-leavers becoming available for white collar jobs. Describing this situation as a 'skills shortage' makes the jobs sound flatteringly high-status. In fact the bulk of them will be jobs that grown men would not take at the wages industry is prepared to pay, which is why, despite the lip-service paid to equal opportunities, they are thought particularly suitable for women. Nevertheless this is a time when the largest pool of under-employed women, those with small children, have bargaining power. It could be used to press for something more family-friendly than workplace daycare.

The public image of daycare is of pre-school children playing together in the nurseries, playgroups and nursery classes that should indeed by available to all. These are the images that inform campaigns for workplace nurseries, but they do not reflect the realities for parents or for children. Reality is taking a baby or toddler twice-daily on a packed commuter-train and then a bus, to a nursery sponsored by work but probably in a lower-rental back-street. It is most unlikely to be close enough for on-demand breast feeding. If it is close enough for lunch-break visits, reality is forgoing lunch-hour shopping for the evening meal and facing an extra 'goodbye'. Most existing workplace nurseries get no daytime visits from parents. Reality is also having a small child's nursery place dependent on parental employment. Tied housing has been frowned upon for years as a potential infringement of workers' liberty; what possesses Trades Unions to smile upon tied nurseries? Children would surely be better-served if industry paid for community-based groups controlled by people (such as parents) who know about childcare.

The popular image of daycare, and the possible use of workplace nurseries, end when children reach school-age, but the problems of combining full time work with parenting do not. School hours do not fill work-hours, especially with a journey at either end; school holidays are at least three times as long as most annual leave entitlements; half-terms, polling and in-service days, not to mention illnesses, make even five consecutive weeks of unbroken school attendance exceptional. The National Out Of School Alliance estimates that one in five children between five and ten years is left alone in the school holidays and comes home in term-time to an empty house. Out of school clubs do vital work but there are only about 300 of them...It is extraordinary that a society professing itself concerned about child protection should ignore this situation, graphically described by one home counties Police Schools Liaison officer: 'I see dozens of five and six years olds finding their own way home. A lot of them are scared to let themselves into dark houses in winter, though they wouldn't tell their mums that. I'm scared for every single one of them: scared of the traffic; scared of the bullies who take their sweet-money and scared of the adults who might harm them.'

If pre-school day-care groups *were* sited in community-centres, they could simultaneously serve as focal points for a comprehensive network of out-of-school and holiday care. Brothers and sisters and local friends would then have a shared base; parents could collect all ages in a single journey and some adults could work part-time in and for their local communities, as people have done with such satisfaction and success within the Pre-School-Playgroups movement.

Current daycare debates do not say much about babies because our few Local Authorities nurseries, and some registered childminders, will only take them under exceptional circumstances so most people assume that they are at home with Mum or maybe with Granny. Reality is different, again. Unregistered minders already take uncounted thousands of infants and some commercially-run daycare centres accept them from as young as six weeks. The Government's Consultation Paper number 2 on the Children Act (Policy and Standards of Day Care and Educational Services [Guidance]) sounds a note of caution about group care for more than twenty hours per week for babies under one year of age, and expresses a vague preference for individual childminding, but then prints guidance applying to all children under two. There is no doubt that as and when workplace nurseries come into existence, there will be babies in them.

Any well-intentioned adult can give a baby adequate care for a couple of hours. That is the (tenuous) justification for using agency babysitters and conference-creches: there may be distress at being left, but not developmental damage. Full-time care, day after day, is dramatically different. Only adults who know, have known and will go on knowing the individual baby can provide the continuous security and consistent responses that optimally build self image and feelings of personal empowerment. And they can only do it for one,

13 Towards a child-friendly society

or maybe two, infants of the same age-stage simultaneously (*pace* mothers of twins but ask anyone with triplets). Of course a baby does not care whether caring people are his or her parents (babies do not know about genetics), but s/he needs a parent-like commitment that is rare outside the vested interests and social expectations of family roles.

It is difficult to see how full-time group care that is economically viable can ever meet these needs of babies and younger toddlers. It certainly does not now. Nursery work is low-paid, low-status and demanding. Employers strive to keep staff by improving their conditions, but every concession to adult needs reduces fulfilment of the children's. Split-shifts to cover the long nursery day reduce adult hours by doubling the number of people with whom babies must interact. Lunch hours, sick leave, holidays and in-service training produce constant staff movement: case-studies suggest that an average of seven different people a day and fifteen a week (some of them strangers 'filling in') may handle each child. And still they leave: the 'mother figure' in charge of each group may change three times in a year.

Individual waged carers are better-placed to meet babies' needs, but that is not something our present society readily acknowledges. After all, one-to-one care by someone outside the family offers no economies of scale. If it releases anyone to fill the skill-shortage it does so only by leaving babies with less-skilled — or at least less well-paid — adults, an uncomfortably colonialist thought. So acknowledgement would mean admitting that where a parent wanted to be at home with a child, s/he was the obvious caretaker and should be economically supported in that choice.

Finding someone who will do, as a job, what we expect mothers to do for love, is not easy, either. Trained resident nannies will not work all day and get up for night feeds and nightmares (let alone clean the house) even for those privileged families who can afford to employ them. A close look at babies' need for individual care suggests that the greatest hope for the children who have least parent-care lies with registered childminders who take them into their family homes. Most do it when their own older children's needs have changed, and not as 'just a job' but to use the skills they have acquired as mothers to finance their continued availability to those children. It is their awareness of their own value as mothers that sometimes enables them to function as substitute mothers. But since these are extra-market values that society does not recognise, childminders are both undermined and underpaid as 'unprofessional' and are therefore often regarded as second best by parents who underrate the importance to their babies of personal relationships and would prefer 'a proper nursery'. The irony is that very few of the people employed in day-care nurseries have NNEB or equivalent qualifications. Recommendations concerning the ratios of adults to children in group care are often largely met by employing sixteen year olds on YTS.

There is no reason why parents — realistically, mothers — should have to choose between being trapped at home with their babies or searching for scarce and usually unsatisfactory daycare. The community-based child centre already postulated to meet the needs of the 2-11s on their own could also meet the needs of babies with adults. Used as a drop-in centre or club by parents and childminders, such a centre could take the isolation and boredom out of being home-based. Adults — both sexes — would get to know each other, each other's children and the professional staff (hopefully local residents and often parents themselves). Babies and toddlers would get to know them too and 'promotion' towards daycare for those whose parents were eager to return to outside work could be gradual and individually paced. In such a setting most babies could be left for a couple of hours occasionally, in an emergency or to give a stressed mother a break. Knowing both the place and the people, many young toddlers could be left part-time, building their confidence and independence towards readiness for longer hours in the pre-school care-group. There are partial models available in the superb 'family centres' run by various children's charities and local authorities, but where those are necessarily open only to families in special difficulty, these would be available as a right to all young families. It is easy to see them at the centre of a wider and wider network; the obvious place for the local toy library, for children's book exhibitions and children's theatre; home base for a Home-Start team; a source of hands-on experience for adolescent parents-to-be, NNEB students, future playgroup leaders and teachers; even a sensible place for an antenatal clinic and for immunisation sessions... Serving the local area and employing local people, such centres could play a major part in giving communities back some sense of themselves as places where people actually live and relate to one another; places where it is actually fun to be home-based with babies. While cost-benefit analysis would present such centres as pipe-dreams because they would cost the Exchequer more money than the present nightmare of having everybody work a 39 hour week and giving tax relief on childcare, there is no doubt that these centres would pay for themselves over time. Reductions in parental stress would probably reduce the rocketing costs of divorce and would certainly lessen child neglect, accidents and abuse. Increases in children's confident happiness would certainly improve their readiness to socialise and learn and might have far-reaching effects on delinquency and eventual educational success. Society prefers to ignore such hard-to-quantify gains but if it is ever to become child-friendly, it must learn (and teach) a new kind of arithmetic.

Children's rights

The more parent-friendly society becomes, the more likely it is that people will enjoy the parenting role; the more they enjoy it, the better they will fill it. But a truly child-friendly society is not simply one in which parents are nice to children. If children's needs are to be met, thus maximising the chances that *their* children's needs will be met in turn, society has to recognise them as real, individual human beings with rights of their own, rather than as appendages of parents who have a right to own them. The benevolent authoritarianism that currently characterises all social policies towards children masks a dangerous refusal to accept that children are people too.

A new recognition of children's rights would immediately give more genuine consideration to their right to be with parents because that is almost invariably what children want. Serving as guardian *ad litem* for a child caught in a custody battle is an agonisingly frustrating task. Even when the child is mature enough and brave enough clearly to state what living and access arrangements s/he would prefer in this traumatic situation, the battle that is fought out in court is a battle between the rights of the parents. And the one who wins 'possession' of the child will be the one whose personal circumstances are socially approved. There are moves to change things. There is, for example, a scheme to teach volunteer solicitors to take Instructions from children: not just to interview them; not just to listen to them, but actually to represent their interests in court as they themselves see them. Proposed changes in divorce law, making the procedure more leisurely and less adversarial, might leave more space for children's rights to be heard and there is some pressure for the Family Courts that could certainly do so, but only a radical change in the importance we ascribe to children's relationships with parents and parent-figures will offer general protection from present social policy. The same 'social policy' which, having decided that children should be adopted only into families with skin colour to match their own, can be interpreted in support of the sudden removal of children from the only people they know and love as parents, shattering their lives because nobody is truly listening to their agonised distress.

It is social policy that in all its dealings with children, society should give priority to 'the best interests of the child'. But who is to judge the 'best interests' of this particular individual if nobody listens to her? And how can she talk, even to people who will listen, if they are forbidden to grant her the professional confidentiality that is the right of every adult? Surely the use made of Childline, anonymous unless the caller wishes it otherwise, is proof enough that, like the rest of us, children in trouble are more likely to confide if they can be sure of keeping control over what happens next. Sometimes we can resolve conflicts between a child's right to confidentiality and our duty to breach it for her protection by persuading the confiding child to talk for herself to the people we must otherwise tell. But as long as society insists on acting 'for' children as objects of concern, against their direct wishes as individual people, the experience of this teacher, made aware of (comparatively minor) sexual abuse, will be commonplace:

> I'd known for days that there was a problem at home and that she was going to tell me what had been going on. I almost prayed she wouldn't because she trusted me to help *in her terms* and if events moved out of her control she would feel it as the ultimate betrayal...That's what happened, of course...She comes to school from her foster home, now, but she doesn't talk any more. I don't think she will ever trust any adult again and certainly we have contributed to that as much as the father.

The benevolent authoritarianism that dominates our attitudes to children as objects of concern does not only frustrate professionals' attempts to work for individual children within their families, it often directly infringes children's human rights in ways that have long been outlawed for adults.

Look, for instance, at equality for adults and children under the law. No adult in this society may be deprived of his liberty unless he has been convicted of a crime and sentenced under due process. But a child may be deprived of his liberty without even a suspicion that he has done anything illegal. He can be put 'in care' for any number of reasons subsumed under headings that suggest it is 'in his best interests' such as that he is in 'moral danger' or 'beyond control'. Being 'in care' is not meant to be imprisonment of course (although it is an equal loss of liberty) but it can easily become so. The child 'in care', still guiltless of any crime, does not have to assault anyone or even try to kill himself before he can find himself locked up. He just has to keep running away until he is placed in a 'children's home' with a secure unit, or even in an adult prison because there is no 'home' that is prepared to take him.

Apart from *habeas corpus*, bodily integrity is an important part of our civil liberties. Peoples' bodies are supposed to belong to themselves. Only under exceptional circumstances and with legal safeguards can any adult be forced to receive even life-saving medical or surgical treatment. We rightly regard the difficult principle of 'informed consent' as so important that even the compulsory HIV testing that might make a real contribution to public health is being strenuously resisted. On the rising tide of concern about the sexual abuse of children, attempts are being made to teach them to protect themselves from potentially abusive contacts by 'saying no'. But even this important work is sabotaged by the hypocrisy of its social context. Children are not being offered a genuine autonomy over their bodies. They are simply being exhorted to refuse contacts of which we disapprove while still being compelled to accept those judged to be 'in their best interests'. How can a humiliating medical examination, often indistinguishable from indecent assault, be in the interests of a child who is not hurt and insists that 'nothing happened'? It may indeed be in the interests of those who wish to prosecute or avoid prosecution but then it is a public health matter and, as with that HIV test, we should ask first and accept a refusal.

The law also protects adult bodies against being hit or physically assaulted by anyone else, however minor the blow and however excellent the motive. Army sergeants may not hit recruits in the interests of discipline and training for the defence of the realm. The police may not strike suspects except in self-defence, even those suspected of heinous crimes. And if family members hit each other during a quarrel in the privacy of their own homes, there is legal recourse for the victim if he or she wants to invoke it, unless, of course, s/he is a child. British law still positively asserts parents' right to administer 'reasonable physical punishment' to their children and nobody knows better than the child protection agencies how arbitrarily that line between 'reasonable' and 'unreasonable' is placed. A five year old dies of 'pain and shock' after being whipped for refusing to spell her name; everyone is horrified. But a Scottish ten year old is severely belted and extensively marked, and the case brought against the mother founders because the judge assesses the punishment as 'entirely reasonable and richly merited'. A teacher alerts the social workers after seeing slight bruising on a six year old who had been 'smacked' with a wooden spoon. The boy and his younger sister are put on the 'at risk' register and the mother's appeal to the High Court is refused by the President of the Family Division...In the terms under which child protection agencies are currently expected to work, that line between 'reasonable' and unreasonable, or abusive punishment is vital, but in terms of the protection of children's rights as people it is the right to hit them at all that is unreasonable.

Children's needs for privileged parents

It is crucial that children should have the same rights all other people take for granted, but because children are very *young* people, with a lot of growing, developing and learning to do through their parents, a truly child-friendly society has to go a giant step further and acknowledge that parents themselves must sometimes be especially privileged because if they get only what they deserve as adults, their children will not always get what they need.

The DHSS rulebook says this couple must go into bed and breakfast accommodation (and lucky to get it, some might add) because the adults became homeless through their own fecklessness, or on purpose. Applied to adults, that rule may be a just way of managing the injustice of our housing shortage. But applied to parents, it condemns children, in our names, to a way of life that we all know is not just depressing, not just inadequate for their needs, but downright dangerous to their health, happiness and development. If families with young children knew that they would get priority re-housing, some might indeed make themselves homeless on purpose. But would they not be right to feel that if anyone must live in damp rooms or cardboard boxes it should not be children? And should they not have priority for the best housing in the first place, especially for the ground floors and gardens that make more difference to children's lives than to anyone else's?

The judge says this woman who got pregnant on remand must go to prison because she has been convicted of a theft for which a non-pregnant woman might have been sent to prison and we cannot have pregnancy seen as a clever way to a non-custodial sentence. Only a (male) judge could possibly imagine that a woman would (or even could) get pregnant for such a reason during a four week remand, but even supposing one did, would it not still be more important to keep that baby out of prison than to put her in?

The government explains that it cannot increase support for mothers on their own lest other women get pregnant for a free ride, or divorce frivolously. They cannot honestly believe that anyone would have a baby or go through the hell of divorce for a few pounds a week, but while they pretend to believe it we condemn those children to a cycle of self-perpetuating poverty which we know will dominate many of their lives throughout childhood and possibly forever.

Putting parents-and-children first

If society could accept the principle of positive discrimination for parents and children together, their daily lives together could often be transformed to the enormous benefit of children and at little or no financial cost.

Children need space to play and space is a scarce commodity,

13 Towards a child-friendly society

especially in our car-choked, dog-loving cities. Where there is a garden in a square there are prohibitions: 'Keep off the grass' and 'No ball games'. They must be addressed to parents and children since dogs don't read. Besides there's smelly evidence that dogs don't keep off that grass and that toddlers had better. No cycling, of course. Bikes might bother more important people, such as employees on their lunch hours. What would it cost to change those notices to read 'Children under twelve and accompanying adults only' and 'No adult admitted unless accompanied by a child'? And what about some more under-fives enclosures in our big parks so a mother, father or minder can relax without losing the child and s/he can run without getting knocked over or falling in a dog's mess?

Our streets are dangerous and polluted places for people who breathe at exhaust-pipe height, but they could be a lot more fun than they are if anybody cared about children's fun. Every railway bridge and building-site hoarding needs viewing slots three feet off the ground because every child needs to see the trains and the bulldozers. Every toddler enjoys posting things so every postbox needs a low slot too. The Post Office tells me children would 'post rubbish' but it is bigger 'children' who post used condoms and fireworks, and anyway, why are there no rubbish bins with proper slots for small children to post their sweet papers? A far cheaper solution to the litter problem than having the Prime Minister pick it up. Some high streets have 'rides' in shop doorways but only where somebody is certain of enough 10p coins from harassed parents to make a big investment worth his while. Children like to climb and sit on things that neither do nor cost anything. A tree stump just outside my favourite greengrocer kept my children beautifully occupied, and a set of library steps and his friendly attitude makes our newsagent a favourite place for local children and even allows their parents to browse among the magazines. Even he does not have a child height section in his counter though.

Children are apprentices to the adult world so the more they go about with adults the better. Entrance charges to museums parents used to visit for their children's sakes should make us all blush. Even the Family Railcards that slash the price of taking several children out miss the real point which is that it should be *cheaper* to take a child than to go alone. Within their local communities, a lot more children would be taken around, perhaps especially by fathers, if it were not so unnecessarily, hurtfully, difficult. Where is a man supposed to take his little girl to pee? And whoever takes her, why are there so few child-sized lavatories or washbasins? And why no dispensers for disposable nappies when they are everywhere for sanitary towels, tampons and condoms? When it comes to facilities in public places, the sparse recognition given to the needs of people using wheelchairs is often greater than that given to the needs of small children in buggies.

Children find it much more difficult than older people to wait their turn. They have to learn, of course, but they do that with their peers, at playgroup age when they can see the point. In the meantime, waiting with a toddler is a major parental stress that is almost completely avoidable. The are special supermarket check-outs for people with fewer than nine items, or for people paying cash, why are there none for people with under-fives? Parents with small children should go first at the doctor's. Why not? Why is it unfair? Somebody has to go first and the waiting room will be more peaceful for everyone if that feverish three year old does not have to wait. And what about that queue at the post-office? And at the bus stop? Airlines load adults with babies and small children first, and into the most convenient seats; why not buses?

The answers, of course, are all the same. In this society children and the people caring for them come last, not first. They come last because children are not seen as real people with equal rights with everyone else and because caring for children is not seen as a real job that is at least as important as any other job. If we could change those attitudes we could glue together the separate projects described in this book to make a structure that would never be swept away. But until we can change them we cannot even ensure that the waitress in that café mops up a child's spill as politely as an adult's and smiles at nursing mothers. Social attitudes sound comfortably distant and theoretical: something other people have and we cannot be responsible for. So when we have played long enough with ideas about making a parent-friendly and therefore a child-friendly society, it is salutary to come down to earth with the realisation that there is no society that is separate from us. The whole complicated, conservative, consumerist collective is nothing but the children we were, the children we have had, the children we are having now and the children they will have in the future. The people who work, care and are cared-for are the same people. There is nobody else to turn that social tide.